# THE
# MODERN WITCH'S
# GUIDE
## TO
## *Natural Magick*

# THE MODERN WITCH'S GUIDE

## TO *Natural Magick*

**60 SEASONAL RITUALS & RECIPES FOR CONNECTING WITH NATURE**

## TENAE STEWART

AUTHOR OF *THE MODERN WITCH'S GUIDE TO MAGICKAL SELF-CARE*

Skyhorse Publishing

# CONTENTS

# CELESTIAL ALCHEMY & NATURAL MAGICK

Natural magick might seem like a contradiction of terms at first glance. Isn't magick inherently *super*natural? In truth, witches and magickal practitioners have worked with the cycles and materia (that's the materials and tools) of nature to bring about their will far back into the depths of time. Magick is not necessarily supernatural at all. In fact, it may be the most natural thing in the world and can be deeply supportive of your overall well-being and self-care.

**Why do we spell "magick" this way?** In the spiritual community, magick is spelled with a k to differentiate spiritual, intuitive magick from magic tricks or illusion.

## MY OWN JOURNEY WITH NATURAL MAGICK

I've been a practicing cottage witch for over a decade, and I work with nature in my own spiritual practice in many different ways. I honor the cycles of the seasons and how they alter and shift the natural world

around me. I honor the cycles of the moon phases and how they impact my emotions and intuition. I work with plants, flowers, herbs, tea, and essential oils to ground these different energies in my real, daily existence. Nature is an important part of my magickal self-care practice, how I nurture and nourish my physical, mental, emotional, and spiritual needs.

In fact, I was drawn to witchcraft in the first place because of these very same seasonal cycles and moon phases. I've always loved the seasons and looked forward to the next one on the horizon. Even as a kid, I loved helping my mom decorate our house for springtime with fresh flowers and bunnies, for autumn with leaves and pumpkins, and for winter with evergreen garlands and sparkling ornaments. Every season also came with its own delicious foods to savor and enjoy: Grandma's deviled eggs and Swiss chard ravioli in springtime, barbecued nectarines in summer, Mom's pumpkin chocolate chip cookies at the very first sign of fall, and the longstanding family recipes for gingerbread cookies and spiked eggnog at the holidays. These are all still recipes I make or enjoy with family every year because, for me, the seasons are deeply rooted in the plants, scents, and flavors that are associated with them.

I also loved the moon as a kid, and that was truly my first foray into witchcraft. The full moon rose right outside the window of my childhood bedroom, and I watched it rise every month in awe. Something about that sight sparked a little bit of magick in me. I began actually practicing magick and witchcraft in college, exploring the seasonal and lunar celebrations before eventually falling off the spiritual bandwagon during my last few years there. At the time, I told myself I was too busy to keep up with my practices, that perhaps being a witch had been a phase and it was something I had outgrown. I intentionally put it on a mental shelf as something I had once done.

But in 2015, my life was turned upside down. I lost my childhood home, beloved pets, and everything I owned, including many precious family heirlooms, in a devastating wildfire. For the first six months after the fire, I sort of drifted. I found an apartment, moved to a much more urban area, got a new job, and experienced radical changes in basically every area of my life.

Through a series of coincidences involving a craft store and a cheap palmistry poster, my curiosity about magick was abruptly sparked again. I quickly realized that what I had needed for the past six months of grief and trauma that I had been navigating was a spiritual anchor. I was completely missing my connection to nature, to the earth, to my intuition, and to something greater than myself. I think that I truly started the post-fire healing process the day I brought home that silly palmistry poster—which still hangs above my altar in honor of that reawakening!

Even in the interim years when I believed I was no longer practicing, I still honored the seasons in so many ways through food, gardening, and a simple awareness of the changes constantly occurring around me in nature. When I recommitted to my spiritual path and reclaimed my inner witch, I started doing those same things with more intention, developing my knowledge around how I could channel the energy of each season with purpose.

## THE SEASONS, MOON PHASES & ASTROLOGY

This book is going to delve into what the cycles of the seasons, moon phases, and astrology are and how you can work with them in witchcraft. Specifically, we will be looking at how you can use herbalism and plants to practice natural magick in alignment with the sun and moon for your overall wellness and self-care. The tools of herbalism, including tea and essential oils, are excellent ways to ground the energy of nature in your life in a really tangible and accessible way.

Let's define the basics right now so we're speaking the same language: There are, of course, four seasons: spring, summer, autumn, and winter. In magick, we can break these seasons down into the eight sabbat festivals and the twelve astrological signs. There are also four moon phases: new, waxing, full, and waning. Each moon phase occurs in a particular astrological sign every month, related to the current season. The movement of the sun and moon through the constellations is all intrinsically interconnected. We experience these cycles as complex, overlapping layers throughout the months and years.

## The Wheel of the Year

Many witches celebrate the seasonal sabbats, which are a set of eight pagan holidays inspired by ancient Celtic and European festivals. Collectively, these holidays are referred to as the Wheel of the Year. Each season contains two sabbats: an equinox or solstice, and a fire festival. The equinoxes and solstices are astronomical events that occur when the sun moves into a specific zodiac sign. The fire festivals, also known as cross-quarter days, are the halfway point of each season and occur on specific calendar dates, although some witches celebrate them astrologically or on the nearest full moon instead.

## Astrological Seasons

The sun moves through all twelve zodiac signs every year, spending about one month in each sign. These astrological seasons always occur at the same time each year and usher in a particular energy and focus for the collective. For example, in the Northern Hemisphere, spring always occurs during Aries, Taurus, and Gemini seasons, which are in late March, April, May, and early June.

## Moon Phases

The moon moves through all twelve zodiac signs every month, spending only about two and a half days in each sign. The new moon happens once a month when the sun and moon are exactly aligned in the same zodiac sign. For example, the new moon in Aries always happens during Aries season in March or April. During this three-day period, the moon appears completely dark. The full moon also happens once a month when the sun and moon are exactly opposite one another in opposite zodiac signs. For example, the full moon in Aries always happens during

Libra season (the opposite sign of the zodiac), in September or October. During this three-day period, the sun shines on the full face of the moon and so it appears completely illuminated. In between, we experience the waxing and waning moons, when the moon appears to be growing bigger until the full moon and then smaller again until the new moon.

# CELESTIAL ALCHEMY

Many witches celebrate the sabbats, honor the moon phases, read their birth charts, and practice astrology as separate tools without ever realizing that these are all part of one larger system. I had been practicing witchcraft for many years before I learned how these systems are interconnected. It was a major lightbulb moment for me and one I knew I had to start sharing with my community of witches. In fact, many of my clients have told me that coming to understand how these different systems are interconnected has helped them feel more confident and clearer in their practices than ever before. If astrology has ever felt confusing or overwhelming for you, learning it as one element of a larger cosmic cycle is probably going to feel surprisingly accessible.

**Astrology is the connecting thread between the seasons and moon phases.** Each of the seasons occurs when the sun is in three specific zodiac signs. Each of the eight sabbats takes place when the sun is in a particular sign and the equinoxes and solstices are actually triggered by the sun moving into a new sign. The new moon can physically only happen when the sun and moon are aligned in the same zodiac sign and the full moon can only happen when they are in opposite signs.

Alchemy is an ancient form of magick and scientific thought that sought to turn common metals such as iron into gold—to transform them from one material into another, more valuable one. Working with the seasons, moon phases, and astrology together can function in much the same way by transforming separate, seemingly unrelated systems and cycles into a larger, unified whole. I like to call my system for learning the seasons, moon phases, and astrology "celestial alchemy," because it's almost like the sun, moon, and planets dance together in the cosmos to become more than the sum of their parts. We also become our most magickal and intuitive selves when we work with them.

This book will guide you through my process of celestial alchemy. But I'm a big believer that information should be actionable and grounded in reality, not just knowledge that floats around in the ether without actually impacting our real, daily lives, which is why this book isn't just going to stop there! The seasons, moon phases, and astrology are three fundamental components of my practice of natural magick (though not all witches work with all or any of these). The fourth leg of natural magick is herbalism because, although the cosmos is the guiding energy of the universe, the way we actually experience them on earth is through Mother Nature.

In every season (which, as you've already learned, includes certain astrological signs, moon phases, and sabbat celebrations), plants clearly express the energy of that season, whether they are blossoming, fruiting, or in hibernation. Plants can also serve as markers of the changing seasons, with some fruits or flowers only in season at certain times of the year. When you work intentionally with these seasonal plants, you can ground the energy of each season and moon phase in reality. Rather than Aries season being an abstract concept, it can be grounded in the plants and fruits that are in season at the spring equinox and in the energy of new ideas and intentions, for example. Even more than that, you can use natural magick and celestial alchemy to better understand your own natural rhythms and, in turn, nurture your own needs meaningfully and intentionally.

But what does it mean to "work with" a plant, exactly? Herbalism has many different forms and faces, ranging from the very technical and advanced to the almost innocuously common. You don't need to have any prior experience with herbalism to access the recipes in this book. We delve into simple, easy practices that you'll be able to do with things you probably already have on hand! There are many wonderful books out there about making tonics, tinctures, and other more advanced herbal concoctions, and I encourage you to explore them if this topic interests you. In this book, though, we'll be focusing on practices such as making your own tea blends, essential oils for anointing and diffusing, and other simple techniques involving fresh and dried plants and essential oils.

At its most essential, natural magick asks us to bring our awareness to the energy of each season. To be in flow with that energy, rather than trying to fight against it. To ground our experience of that energy in something tangible that can help us be mindful and present with the energy in our real, daily lives. To take the concepts of energy and magick from the abstract to the accessible. This book is going to guide you in this process of awareness, flow, grounding, and alchemy to help you embrace natural magick in *your* real, daily life. So, let's dive in!

# Chapter 1
# HERBALISM & MAGICKAL CORRESPONDENCES

Natural magick is all about being in flow with the cycles of nature and utilizing nature's tools to get grounded, nourish yourself, and manifest your desires. Over the next few chapters, we are going to look at the cycles of the moon and the seasons and explore how they impact you personally. But before we venture into the stars, let's spend a little time right here on earth.

The primary tools of natural magick are plants and crystals. Both are of the earth and the soil and can be used to ground your intentions, desires, and magick in the real, tangible world. In this book, we'll be working with mostly plants in a variety of forms, including fresh, dried, flowers, roots, leaves, and essential oils, though we will also work with crystals to amplify the energy of our herbal allies.

Herbalism is the practice of working with plants for healing and wellness. There are many different ways to utilize the energy of plants to ally with their natural and magickal properties. Essential oils are the

most potent of these, representing the most highly concentrated form of each plant, and can be diluted in water or oil in a variety of forms. On the other end of the spectrum, flower essences and crystal elixirs are made from flowers and crystals submerged in water, then strained, or even from dew collected from flower petals, with the merest suggestion of actual plant or mineral material.

My personal favorite form of herbalism is making handmade tea blends with unique combinations of tea leaves, herbs, and flowers. Served hot or iced, tea is a lovely, calming way to introduce both the healing and metaphysical impact of plants into your body and connect with the cyclical rhythms of nature.

Whatever form your herbalism takes and whatever types of potions you're brewing up, working with plants and crystals is a powerful way to ground your spiritual experience in the real world. The cycles and systems that draw so many witches to our paths are those of the cosmos—the cycles of the sun and the seasons, the cycles of the moon phases, and even the cycles of the planets as they move through the astrological signs. All of these are beautiful and impact us in real, meaningful ways, but they're still somehow outside of ourselves.

If you've ever struggled to conceptualize exactly how the moon phases affect your emotions or how to celebrate an ancient harvest festival in the twenty-first century, working with plants and natural magick can help bridge that gap. It's easiest to see with the seasons, of course (certain plants are in season at certain times of the year, and we naturally gravitate toward them at those times, like pumpkins in fall or daffodils in spring), but this applies to the moon phases and astrology as well, as each plant is associated with particular signs of the zodiac, elements, and properties that can help us align with the corresponding energies of the moon and planets. Not only can natural magick make the moon phases, sabbats, and astrology more accessible, but it can also help you use them in meaningful ways for your ultimate wellness and self-care. As you consume or absorb energy from a plant, you sync up with its corresponding energy in the cosmos as well. As above, so below.

In this chapter, we are going to explore how to practice some basic forms of herbalism including tea and tisane blending, diffusing essential oils, anointing with oils, and infusing salts, sugars, oils, and more. You'll also find profiles of twelve plants we will work with in this book and their corresponding magickal properties.

## SEASONAL, LUNAR & ASTROLOGICAL HERBALISM

Plants are your allies in magick and self-care, providing healing medicine for your body, mind, heart, and soul. The plant allies you feel called to work with likely shift throughout the month and year, depending on the moon phase and season. This is your body and intuition crying out for connection to the cosmic cycles. There are a number of different ways you can choose to align with these cycles through plant allies and natural magick, both intuitively and intentionally.

Sometimes you will want to just surrender to the plants that seem to call to you—a little like the intuitive eating practice of trusting that your body knows what nutrients you need most from day to day. At other times, you will want to work intentionally with plant allies that align with the moon phase and season in order to harness and channel their power and receive their gifts!

## Magickal Correspondences of Plants

Every plant has what are known as correspondences, a list of energies and concepts that it is associated with. These correspondences, or properties, can be related to the plant's appearance, cultivation or habitat, taste or scent, what part of the body it is used to treat, and folkloric and magickal associations.

Correspondences are essentially the foundation of this book. I'm going to be sharing correspondences for each of the moon phases, seasons, sabbat celebrations, and astrological signs. I'll also be sharing recipes using those corresponding plants to help you celebrate and honor each of these celestial events. All of the moon phases, seasons, sabbats, and signs have corresponding plants, as well as corresponding crystals, colors, goddesses, tarot cards, and more. Although our primary focus will be on plants, I'll be sharing some or all of these correspondences for each aspect of the celestial wheel.

Correspondences might seem like a completely esoteric mystery at first. These are not hard and fast rules by any means, but there is actually some rhyme *and* some reason to them! There are some excellent correspondence reference books out there that you can refer to, but let's first break down *why* certain plants are associated with certain properties.

## A NOTE ON GODDESSES

I've made an effort to share corresponding goddesses from a variety of cultures and pantheons throughout this book, as representation is very important! However, it's important to do your own research before calling on a deity and to work with them in meaningful and respectful ways. That includes respecting the cultures they originate from and being actively anti-cultural appropriation in your practice. It is possible to work with a goddess from another culture in an appreciative, *not* appropriative way, but this must be done with intention, respect, and even reparations where necessary.

First, we start with the elements: plants are usually associated with one of the four elements of fire, earth, air, and water.

- Fire plants are typically spicy, spiky, poisonous, or otherwise "hot" in some way.
- Earth plants are usually those that grow underground (like tubers), that we primarily use the roots of, or that are deeply grounding in some way.
- Air plants might be very fragrant, as their scent is carried to us on the breeze, or bend and sway in the wind rather than breaking or standing firm.
- Water plants are usually composed of a high-water content (like aloe) or grow in water (like lotus). They might also be

night-blooming—since they bloom in the moonlight and the moon's gravitational pull impacts the element of water on earth!

As you can see, determining a plant's elemental ruler is actually fairly easy, even with very little esoteric knowledge.

Next, we look to the plant's planetary and astrological rulership. That might sound complicated, but once you're familiar with a few basic astrological concepts, this can be easy to figure out as well. Each planet in our solar system, as well as the sun and moon, are associated with one or two of the elements and one or two astrological signs in the zodiac. When you've identified the elemental ruler of a plant, it narrows down the possibilities of cosmic rulership by quite a bit.

- The sun is connected to the element of fire and rules the sign of Leo.
- The moon is connected to the element of water and rules the sign of Cancer.
- Mercury is connected to the element of air and sometimes earth and rules the signs of Gemini and Virgo.
- Venus is connected to the elements of earth, air, and sometimes water, and rules the signs of Taurus and Libra.
- Mars is connected to the element of fire and rules the sign of Aries.
- Jupiter is connected to the element of fire and rules the sign of Sagittarius.
- Saturn is connected to the element of earth and rules the sign of Capricorn.
- Uranus is connected to the element of air and rules the sign of Aquarius.
- Neptune is connected to the element of water and rules the sign of Pisces.
- Pluto is connected to the element of water and rules the sign of Scorpio.

Let's take lavender as an example. If you know that lavender is very fragrant, you know that it's probably an air plant, and in turn, you know it's likely ruled by either Mercury or Uranus.

Although some plants are ruled by Uranus, Neptune, and Pluto, these three planets were not discovered until the eighteenth, nineteenth and twentieth centuries, so most plants are traditionally considered to be ruled by the seven other celestial bodies in our solar system. That's because most correspondences are connected to ancient traditions that were long established before the discovery of these so-called "modern" planets. Therefore, with a traditional plant like lavender, we know that it's ruled by Mercury and Mercury's air sign, Gemini.

Don't worry if you feel stumped by this. It's 100 percent acceptable to refer to books of correspondences to determine or confirm elemental, planetary, and astrological rulership. But I do encourage you to play with this exercise and start learning to identify rulership based on the appearance, taste, scent, and habitat of plants that you encounter! It's also totally okay to choose to work with a plant based on your intuition. Even if every correspondence book you can find says that lavender is ruled by Mercury, but you feel like it helps you connect with the energy of the moon, follow your intuitive instinct.

In addition to their elemental, planetary, and astrological correspondences, most plants are also associated with particular magickal intentions or outcomes. This might be based on the plant's therapeutic qualities, its use as a remedy for certain illnesses or ailments, folklore or tradition, or even sympathetic associations based on shape and color (such as heart-shaped hawthorn being associated with heart-opening magick).

## Intentional Alignment

Armed with this powerful knowledge of the magickal correspondences of our plant allies, you can intentionally choose to work with plants that align with the energy of a particular moon phase, the moon in a particular sign, a particular astrological transit, or an entire season. (In fact, that's exactly what we'll be doing for the vast majority of this book!) This can be as simple as eating seasonal foods. As I mentioned earlier in this chapter, we are naturally drawn to work with certain plants during each time of the year because they have exactly the medicine (physically and spiritually) that we are in need of during that season. There are no coincidences in nature. For example, fresh greens and herbs are in season in the spring when we are in need of their vibrant energy to kick-start a new year, while tubers and hearty vegetables are in season in the winter when we need their warming support.

You can align your herbalism and natural magick practices with the energy of the cosmos in deeper ways by working with correspondences. To align with the current moon phase, you might choose a plant based on its element. We'll talk more about what the moon phases are and the energy of each in Chapter 2 on page 41, but, as you have already learned, there are four basic moon phases: the new moon, waxing moon, full moon, and waning moon. Of course, there are also four elements, so this is an easy one!

- The new moon is supported by air plants that inspire your new intentions.
- The waxing moon is supported by fire plants that give you energy and motivation.
- The full moon is supported by water plants that nurture your intuition.
- The waning moon is supported by earth plants that ground you.

The moon moves through all twelve signs of the zodiac each month, so you can align with the energy of each moon sign by choosing a plant ruled by that sign. The same goes for the sun's astrological seasons. The sun spends about one month in every sign each year, which is an ideal time to work with the plants of that sign for a more extended period of immersion.

You can also work with plants that help you align with planetary transits, the movement of the planets through the twelve signs of the zodiac. For example, when Venus moves into her home sign of Taurus, you might choose to work with plants ruled by Venus for self-love spells and to open the heart, as those energies will already be cosmically present. By working with plants that align with the current lunar, solar, and astrological energies around us, you can both channel their power as a boost to your own magickal workings and ground the experience of them in your tangible reality.

## Intuitive Alignment

In astrology, the moon rules your emotions and intuition, so it can have a profound impact on your mood and energy level. The moon cycle is also roughly the same length as an average menstrual cycle, about twenty-eight days. A popular, simple, yet very powerful practice is tracking your moods, emotions, energy levels, and menstrual cycles (if applicable), with the four moon phases. I highly recommend tracking your moods with the moon, as it can really help you understand the ebb and flow of your own emotions and energy levels, which are probably not nearly as random as you might sometimes think.

You can also track your intuitive alignment with the moon cycle through the plants you feel called to under each phase and sign. This can be a really fun exercise to tune into your own personal associations with plants and to develop your own correspondences. Every few days, intuitively choose a tea blend or an essential oil to work with and note what plants you chose, as well as what phase and sign the moon is in. This isn't a one-and-done experience—very little in nature ever is—so I recommend tracking for at least two months to see if any patterns emerge.

Although the plants you may be drawn to during certain signs or phases might not be "officially" or traditionally associated with those signs and phases, this will help you start to develop your own correspondences and connection with your plant allies. There is no wrong answer in natural magick or witchcraft. Write your own rules and traditions if you feel called to!

For the rest of this book, we'll be focusing mostly on intentional alignment of plants with the sun, moon, and planets, but I encourage you to practice intuitive alignment as well. The most powerful magick is truly a combination of both intention and intuition.

## Substitutions & Replacements

Now, sometimes, you might come across a recipe or spell that includes an ingredient you don't want to use for one reason or another. Some essential oils are quite expensive, and you might want to use a more affordable option, you might not have a given ingredient on hand, or you might be allergic to or simply dislike the taste or smell of something. For example, I happen to be allergic to chamomile, which is frequently recommended for sleep, meditation, and dream work.

Whatever your reason for wanting to replace or omit an ingredient in a recipe or spell, I want you to feel 100 percent confident in doing so! You can always substitute an herb, flower, fruit, or oil for *any* reason. You can do this intentionally by checking what other plants are associated with similar magickal purposes or have similar scents or tastes, or you can do this intuitively simply by choosing another plant that you feel drawn to.

You can also always omit an ingredient. For example, if a diffuser blend calls for three different essential oils and you only have two of them, just include those two. You are by no means obligated to create a recipe or spell exactly as it is written in this book or in any book, nor do you have to run out and buy a million ingredients just for one recipe. You make the rules in your own practice!

## HERBALISM TOOLS, TECHNIQUES & SAFETY

You won't need a lot of tools to make most of the recipes in this book— just commonly found fresh and dried herbs and flowers and essential oils—but a few implements will be helpful:

- **Mortar and pestle:** A stone bowl for grinding spices and combining ingredients.
- **Glass jars and bottles:** All different sizes for storing dried herbs and spices, as well as storing your own concoctions.
- **Roller ball bottles:** Tall, thin, glass bottles with a metal ball topper.
- **Spray bottles:** Glass bottles fitted with a spray cap for cleansing sprays, toners, etc.
- **Pipettes:** Plastic droppers for transferring carrier oils and essential oils into your chosen container.
- **Tea infusers:** Metal or rubber mesh containers to infuse tea into hot water.
- **Tea bags:** Empty mesh paper bags that can be filled with tea, tied, then placed into hot water.
- **Carrier oils:** Neutral oils such as vegetable, olive, canola, sunflower, or almond that can be used to dilute essential oils.
- **Epsom salts:** A chemical compound of magnesium sulfate that's often used for soaking, bathing, and relaxation.

# TEAS & TISANES

Blending teas is my favorite herbalism activity and a big part of my own spiritual practice. There's something so magickal and witchy about mixing flowers and herbs together, *a little of this and a little of that,* then brewing a warm, cozy cup and curling up in my favorite chair to enjoy it. And it really is that easy! Making your own tea blends is a great way to get started with herbalism in a super accessible format.

One thing to know first, though, is that many tea blends are not actually tea at all! The word "tea" refers to a cup brewed with a specific plant, *Camellia sinensis,* which is native to Asia, especially China and India. Black, green, and white tea leaves are all made from the leaves of this plant that are processed and dried in different ways. If a tea contains plant material that is not from *Camellia sinensis,* like most herbal and floral tea blends, it is actually called a *tisane,* though this term is not very commonly used.

Blending your own teas is surprisingly easy. I remember being shocked at how easy it was when I first learned, as I drink a *lot* of tea. Being able to make my own has saved me a lot of time and money over the years! You can make tea from pretty much any plant that's not poisonous or toxic to humans, though some will certainly taste better than others. Your choices will be decided by the purpose of the tea: is it to align with a particular season or moon phase? Is it to support some kind of magickal intention you want to create or receive? Is it a healing remedy? Or is it just to enjoy?

Once you've settled on a purpose for your tea blend, keep the blending pyramid in mind. At the widest part of the pyramid is the base of your tea. The base usually makes up the largest part of the blend and might be black, green, or white tea leaves or a flower or herb, such as rose or lavender, that's fairly substantial and has a distinctive flavor. The next portion of the pyramid is the supporting elements of your tea blend.

These are the elements that add flavor, structure, and magick to your blend but aren't too overpowering. Supporting elements might be flowers with a gentler flavor like jasmine or soft spices like cardamom. Finally, the top of the pyramid is the accent of your tea blend. This is usually a smaller amount of a plant that has a strong flavor or magickal property, so you don't want too much of it! The accent shouldn't take over the blend but rather add just the right finishing note to complete the flavor profile and magickal intention. Accents might be potent spices like cinnamon, peppercorns, or ginger, or vibrant flowers like hibiscus.

Your magickal tea blend should feel aligned with your intentions and preferably taste delicious (although some healing remedies might be good for you but not taste great). It's not important that you follow the pyramid exactly or perfectly identify whether a component of your blend is supporting or an accent. It's also not important that you memorize the magickal properties of every plant out there, or even necessarily of every plant in your kitchen, as your own instincts and intuition will guide you as to which plants to choose. What's more important is that you feel confident and comfortable combining plants based on your enjoyment of them and the magickal intention you associate with them.

In this book, you'll find that most of the tea recipes are written in "parts." This gives you the ratio of ingredients to one another so that you can make as much or as little of the recipe as you need. One tablespoon total of plant material is ideal for a single cup of tea, while 3 to 4 tablespoons is ideal for a pot of tea.

## Tea Rituals

As you consume a cup of tea, whether it be your own blend or a store-bought blend that you enjoy, you are inviting the magick of the plants—and of the energies, elements, and astrological signs and planets associated with them—into your own body.

In fact, it's then possible to take the spiritual experience of that cup of tea one step further with a ritual. Tea rituals are prevalent in cultures all over the world. The most famous is the Japanese tea ceremony, which is dedicated to simplicity, finely controlled movements, and delicate matcha tea made with a wooden whisk. The entire tea ceremony is a moving meditation. In India, tea is called chai and is made with black tea leaves and warm, inspiring spices like cinnamon and peppercorns. It's also often mixed with milk for a delicious latte.

**"Chai tea" is actually redundant, as the word chai means tea in many languages.** That "chai tea" latte is really just a chai latte—a personal favorite of mine!

There are also tea rituals found in China, India, the Middle East, and North Africa, many of which are focused on reverence for spirit, ancestors, or elders or are rooted in social customs and respect for one another. There are also rituals involving other sacred beverages made from plants like kava in Fiji and cacao in Central and South America. Although the actual materials, plants, and movements involved differ widely, there is something universally sacred about steeping or extracting the essence of a plant in order to prepare a warm beverage, then sipping it in a reverent and ritualistic manner. In this type of experience, you are calling on the plant as an ally to support and nourish your body, mind, and intuition.

Your own tea ritual could be focused on meditation, relaxation, energizing your body, uplifting your mind, connecting with your intuition, honoring spirit or your ancestors, receiving the wisdom of your plant allies, or connecting with those close to you. Tea rituals can be small, sacred moments or long stretches devoted to self-care and mindfulness.

- **Choose Your Focus.** To formulate a tea ritual of your own, start by considering the function and purpose of the ritual. What intention would you like to set?
- **Choose Your Plant Allies.** Once you have an idea of the vibe you'd like to cultivate, choose the plants to include in your tea blend. For example, if you're looking for a heart-opening, meditative experience, you might go with rose and cacao, but you're probably not going to choose something spicy or energizing like peppercorns. If you're looking for a way to connect with your intuition, you might choose mugwort or lavender, but probably not something deeply grounding and earthy like dandelion root or burdock.

- **Choose Your Setting.** The environment of your tea ritual can be very important, especially if you're devoting more time to the ritual. If your ritual is more of a mini, on-the-go experience, this will have less bearing but is still a factor to consider! Just like with the plants you've chosen, you want to align the setting of your ritual with your intention. Sipping tea outside in the garden or at the park is going to be a different experience than sitting at your altar on a meditation pillow. With our example of a heart-opening meditative tea ritual, you might want that very sacred, luscious, goddess setting at your altar. But if your tea ritual is more about finding inner peace while stuck in traffic on your morning commute, then the car is a totally acceptable setting, too.

- **Choose Your Actions.** The "action" of a tea ritual can be as simple as becoming aware of the heat of the mug on your palms, watching the steam curl in the air above it, and lifting it to your lips for a quiet, reverent sip. This mini ritual can be a moment of mindfulness in the middle of your morning beauty routine, lunch-packing chaos, or workday.

You can extrapolate on this most simplistic version of a tea ritual and incorporate the act of choosing the plants, mixing the blend, boiling the water, brewing the tea, or pouring water over the tea leaves into your cup—or all of the above! As with any type of ritual, I encourage you to choose actions that feel meaningful to you and that you can really bring your attention and focus to. Don't feel like you have to make this entire process into a ritual if it feels like too much, inaccessible, or not interesting to you. Rituals should not be meaningless activities that you just go through the motions of, but rather truly sacred pauses to reflect, connect, and release.

# ESSENTIAL OILS

Essential oils are the most potent form of plant material, as they contain a very high concentration of the plants they are made from. They represent the very essence of the plant—the essence of its fragrance, healing power, and magickal gifts. I love using essential oils in natural magick because they can be so uplifting and a great option for working with plants in a subtle, modern way. There are four basic ways to work with essential oils: inhaling, diffusing, anointing, and infusing.

## ESSENTIAL OIL SAFETY

It's important to be sure that the oils you're using are actually essential and not fragrance oils, which often contain chemicals and sometimes do not even contain any actual plant material. Many brands promote their essential oils as "therapeutic grade," but there are no specific guidelines for this and no governing body that oversees it, so bear this in mind. Most scientists and aromatherapists agree that essential oils should not be consumed, even if some brands promote them for internal use. It's also important to do your research on which oils are safe for children, pets, and pregnant individuals, as due to their high potency and concentration, some oils can be toxic when diffused or applied.

## Inhaling

Inhaling is certainly the easiest way to work with essential oils. You simply inhale the scent of the essential oil directly from the bottle or from your hands. You can hold the bottle a few inches from your nose or place a few drops of oil in the palm of your hands, rub them together, then cup them a few inches from your nose to inhale the fragrance. This can be a fast and very soothing way to receive some of the benefits of essential oils. That said, it's very important to be aware of which oils might be irritating to your skin before inhaling from your hands, as well as to note that for those with asthma or sensitive respiratory tracks, inhaling certain pungent oils like eucalyptus can be harmful.

## Diffusing

Diffusing is perhaps the most common method of working with essential oils. Simply place a few drops of the oils of your choice into a diffuser and allow them to naturally fill the air with their scent. Reed diffusers and salt diffusers are very low-tech options that you can even make yourself, while electric ultrasonic diffusers create a fine mist of essential oils diluted in water, which can also act as a humidifier. Diffusing is perfect for filling your sacred space, home, or office with the magick, energy, and aromatherapeutic benefits of essential oils.

## Anointing

Anointing is another method for working with essential oils and is perhaps the witchiest of the options. Anointing is the process of rubbing oil on an object or person in order to imbue it with power, often done in a ceremonial way. It's common for witches to anoint candles for spellwork or to anoint our own bodies.

Anointing candles is a great way to add power and focus to your candle spells, one of the simplest and most accessible types of spells. All you really need to perform a candle spell is a candle, something to light it with, and an intention, but you can add additional ingredients to your spell to boost its power. Some of the most common ingredients to add to candle spells include herbs and oils.

One option is to simply rub a carrier oil (a plain, unscented oil such as vegetable, olive, or sunflower oil) on your candle, then sprinkle herbs on it or roll it in dried herbs or ground spices that align with your intention. For example, for a self-love spell, you might roll your oiled candle in dried, crushed rose petals, or for a success spell, you might use ground cinnamon and cloves.

Another option is to make a special anointing oil blend for your candle spell. For this, you'll want to blend a carrier oil with essential oils that align with your intention. This is a similar idea but longer lasting, so it's a great option for long-term candle spells where you intend to burn the candle again and again over time. Simply combine the essential oils in a small bowl and dip your fingers in it to rub on the candle or make ahead of time and store in a bottle fitted with a roller ball cap.

You can also anoint *yourself* with oils! Anointing myself is one of my favorite ways to work with essential oils because it is such a personal and intimate magickal experience. Due to their very high potency, it's important to dilute essential oils in a carrier oil before applying them to your skin. Your dilution ratio will likely be between 2–3 percent essential oil to carrier oil, though it could be slightly lower depending on your personal preference. Also note that some essential oils should generally not be applied to the skin, including citrus oils, spice oils, and even mint oils for those with sensitive skin.

Anointing with oils is an ancient ritual in many different spiritual traditions, so this method is good for especially sacred circumstances—which you probably have a lot more of than you might think. I like to anoint with diluted lavender oil every night before bed, for example, to wind down my evening in a sacred, relaxing, and intuitive way. Your morning ritual could include a self-love anointing oil to start your day on a loving note. Other opportunities to work with anointing oils include rituals to honor a particular goddess using oils made from plants associated with her, before a sacred self-pleasure or sex magick experience, or as part of your sabbat or moon phase rituals.

Roller ball bottles are ideal for storing anointing oils, as they are made for rolling onto skin. Some common places to anoint yourself include your wrists, behind your ears, your third eye (the space between and just above your eyes), and your sternum.

## Infusing

Finally, you can also use essential oils to infuse bath salts, soaps, and candles. Infusing bath salts is probably the simplest bath product you can make at home—and therefore my favorite! All you need are Epsom salts and your favorite essential oils, though you can add other types of salts or dried herbs as well.

# HERBAL & CRYSTAL INFUSIONS

You can also make infusions of sea salt, sugars, cooking oils, honey, and even liquors, in which case you're infusing with fresh or dried herbs instead of essential oils. To infuse salts and sugars, just mix the salt or sugar and dried herbs together and store in a jar for a few weeks to absorb the flavors. Infused salts are delicious with savory herbs like rosemary, sage, or thyme while infused sugars can be made with sweeter or more citrusy herbs like mint or lemon verbena, flowers like rose or lavender, or whole spices like cinnamon or cloves. To infuse liquids like cooking oils, honey, and liquor, rinse your herbs, then pat dry or hang them to dry beforehand, as you don't want to introduce a lot of water into your infusion. Place the dried herbs inside a tall glass bottle or medium-large mason jar and fill with oil, honey, vodka, or gin. Allow to infuse for a few weeks, then strain the herbs out.

Another type of infusion is an elixir, which is made by infusing a natural material into water that is meant to be consumed. By this definition, teas and tisanes are also elixirs, though we don't commonly use this word for them. In natural magick, we most often see this in reference to crystal elixirs, which are water infused with the energy and vibration of crystals and stones. Just like plants, crystals are natural materials from the earth that correspond to certain energies— rose quartz for love and amethyst for intuition, for example. To make a crystal elixir, simply place a non-toxic, water-safe crystal in a glass or jar of water. Allow the crystal to infuse the water with its energy for a few minutes or hours and remove the crystal before consuming the water.

**Do your research and be absolutely certain that the crystal you're choosing to work with is non-toxic and water safe.** A few crystals that are safe to use are rose quartz, clear quartz, amethyst, and citrine. A few crystals that should definitely not be used in this way are selenite, pyrite, moonstone, and lapis lazuli.

You can raise the vibration and refine the focus of any of these infusions by holding your hands on either side of the container, closing your eyes (and opening your third eye), and focusing deeply on your intent. You can imagine a golden or colored light swirling between your hands, filling the infusion with magick or creating a protective shield around it. You might also speak an affirmation or spell over the infusion to increase its power through your words and the vibration of your voice.

# ASTROLOGICAL PLANT ALLIES

In the realm of natural magick, we think of plants as living, breathing entities that carry great wisdom and power within them. This is why plants are our allies. When you choose to work with a plant in this magickal and energetic way, you are choosing to ally with the plant's power, not simply to use or take it. On the following pages, you will find profiles of twelve plants commonly used in natural magick and herbalism. I've chosen one plant to represent each of the twelve zodiac signs and have also shared some alternative plants and substitutions for each sign. We'll be working with these and much more later in this book.

## Pepper

Peppers are found almost universally in cuisine around the world, so it's fitting that we should start here. Whether we're talking bell peppers, jalapeño peppers, ghost peppers, or peppercorns, there's a place for peppers in everything from salsa to curry to tea. In this case, we're primarily talking about peppercorns, which are often black but can also be white, green, or pink, although Aries and Mars rule peppers of all kinds.

Aries is the sign of the fierce, fearsome Warrior and rules most spicy plants, as they attack our taste buds! Peppers and other spicy Aries plants are excellent for magick around physical and psychic protection, as they are energetically on guard as well. Pepper is great for inspiring you to action and for lighting a fire under you when you're in need of some motivation or inspiration.

**Latin Name:** *Piper nigrum*

**Folk Names:** Black pepper, peppercorns

**In Season:** Year-round

**Element:** Fire

**Ruling Sign:** Aries

**Ruling Planet:** Mars

**Magickal Properties:** Protection, dispels negativity

**Parts of Plant Used:** Peppercorns

**Magickal Substitutions:** Any type of pepper, mustard, horseradish, turmeric

**Other Aries Plants:** Mustard, cayenne, cactus

To help you connect with pepper as a plant ally, reflect on the following prompts:

What boundaries of protection can pepper help me set in my life?

_____

_____

_____

How can pepper inspire me to take empowered, aligned action?

_____

_____

_____

## Rose

Rose is one of the most versatile and powerful plants in our self-love arsenal as witches. Its key magickal property is that it supports and aids in opening the heart. Whether you're wanting to call in a new romantic relationship, bring down the walls you've built around your true self, or learn to open yourself up to your intuition, rose is there to help.

Their sweet scent and beautiful blossoms might be considered something of a cliché in the twenty-first century, but roses are a classic symbol of lovers for a reason. Whether you're working with the petals, buds, or fruit that grows just beneath the petals (called rose hips), roses have been associated with love and love goddesses like Venus back into the depths of history. It's worth remembering, however, that roses also have thorns, and that an open, loving heart is not the same thing as being passive or making people-pleasing sacrifices that don't truly align with your soul.

**Latin Name:** *Rosa damascena* or *Rosa centifolia*

**Folk Names:** Rose Otto, attar of rose, Turkish rose, cabbage rose, Rose de Provence

**In Season:** Late spring and early summer

**Element:** Water

**Ruling Sign:** Taurus

**Ruling Planet:** Venus

**Magickal Properties:** Opening the heart, love, beauty, passion, fertility, intuition

**Parts of Plant Used:** Buds, petals, oil, thorns, rose hips

**Magickal Substitutions:** Geranium, hibiscus

**Other Taurus Plants:** Strawberry, apple, birch, oats

To help you connect with rose as a plant ally, reflect on the following prompts:

What do I truly, deeply wish to open my heart to?

_____

_____

_____

How can rose help me bring greater sweetness and pleasure into my life?

_____

_____

_____

## Lavender

Lavender's fragrance has been renowned for millennia. All the way back to Greek and Roman times, lavender was used to perfume soaps and laundry. Whether our intentions are healing, cosmetic, or magickal, we use lavender for much of the same purposes today. Its calming scent is perfect for relaxation and sleep, helping connect you to your dreams and intuition.

As a Mercury-ruled plant, lavender not only helps you align with your own intuitive wisdom, but it also helps you navigate and make sense of the intuitive information you receive. Lavender dissipates confusion and frustration, allowing clarity and your own inner knowing to come to the forefront. Lavender is also lovely for spells and magickal workings around inner and outer peace, love, calm, and even release of control.

**Latin Name:** _Lavandula angustifolia_
**Folk Names:** English lavender

**In Season:** Early- to mid-summer

**Element:** Air

**Ruling Sign:** Gemini

**Ruling Planet:** Mercury

**Magickal Properties:** Calming, sleep, dreams, intuition, purification, love

**Parts of Plant Used:** Flowers, oil

**Magickal Substitutions:** Elder, thyme, valerian

**Other Gemini Plants:** Bergamot, peppermint, lemon verbena

To help you connect with lavender as a plant ally, reflect on the following prompts:

Where in my life can lavender help me find mental peace and clarity?

_____

_____

_____

How does lavender aid me in connecting with and interpreting my intuition?

_____

_____

_____

## Jasmine

The heady, sweet scent of jasmine flowers in bloom is a hallmark of warm summer evenings. Jasmine is ruled by the moon, partly due to the fact that it blooms at night, under the light of the moon herself, and is therefore associated with all the activities of the night: sleep, dreams, and lust. It is excellent for helping you connect with your intuition and to float on the warm, nurturing tide of Cancer season.

The moon also rules your emotional intelligence and how you process and express emotions. Jasmine can help you find inner peace, promote peace in the world around you, and honor your emotions as a core aspect of your overall health and wellness.

**Latin Name:** *Jasminum officinale*

**Folk Names:** Summer jasmine, poet's jasmine, jessamine

**In Season:** Late spring and summer

**Element:** Water

**Ruling Sign:** Cancer

**Ruling Planet:** Moon

**Magickal Properties:** Love, sleep, dreams, divination, emotional health, peace, lust, sensuality

**Parts of Plant Used:** Flowers, oil

**Magickal Substitutions:** Gardenia, lotus, camellia

**Other Cancer Plants:** Eucalyptus, willow, aloe, succulents

To help you connect with jasmine as a plant ally, reflect on the following prompts:

What darkest parts of myself can jasmine gently illuminate like moonlight?

_____

_____

_____

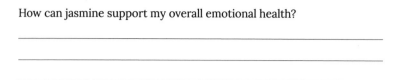

How can jasmine support my overall emotional health?

_____

_____

_____

## Cinnamon

It's said that scent is one of the most powerful triggers for memory. For many of us, the scent of cinnamon triggers memories of cozy, childhood days and delicious, fresh-baked cookies. Cinnamon is a spice made from the sweet, dried bark of a tree native to Southeast Asia. It's commonly used in chai, yummy baked goods, and even savory dishes.

Magickally, cinnamon is all about power—a boost of potency and inspiration to any project or spell. Just as cinnamon is both sweet and spicy, the power it can lend to a magickal working can be both playful and potent. Ruled by the sun, cinnamon is a useful ally for boosting confidence and success of all kinds.

**Latin Name:** _Cinnamomum verum_

**Folk Names:** Sweet wood

**In Season:** Year-round

**Element:** Fire

**Ruling Sign:** Leo

**Ruling Planet:** Sun

**Magickal Properties:** Success, power, protection, prosperity, inspiration, creativity

**Parts of Plant Used:** Bark, leaves, oil

**Magickal Substitutions:** Ginger, nutmeg, allspice

**Other Leo Plants:** Calendula, sunflower, chamomile

To help you connect with cinnamon as a plant ally, reflect on the following prompts:

How does spicy cinnamon inspire self-confidence within me?

_____

_____

_____

What do success and prosperity mean to me?

_____

_____

_____

## Mint

Mint comes in many varieties, but all are known for their fresh, invigorating scent. I'm very lucky to have it growing wild in my backyard, but it's remarkably easy to cultivate in small pots as well. There's something incredibly magickal and witchy about the way it survives (and thrives) just about anywhere—a commentary on our own ability to thrive in unlikely circumstances.

Mint is one of those universal magickal tools that can be used for lots of different purposes. One of its most powerful purposes is for gaining clarity. Even just a deep breath of its pungent scent can clear the mind (and the sinuses). Technically, mint is ruled by Mercury, which rules both Gemini and Virgo. In this case, I've listed mint as a Virgo herb because I find its clarifying properties and ability to help us discern order from chaos to be a very Virgoan quality.

**Latin Name:** *Mentha spicata*

**Folk Names:** Garden mint, balm mint, brandy mint, sage of Bethlehem

**In Season:** Spring through fall

**Element:** Air

**Ruling Sign:** Virgo

**Ruling Planet:** Mercury

**Magickal Properties:** Money, travel, protection, banishing, clarity, concentration, inspiration

**Parts of Plant Used:** Leaves, oil

**Magickal Substitutions:** Any type of mint, (i.e., peppermint, spearmint, etc.), dill, lavender, marjoram

**Other Virgo Plants:** Clover, fern, fennel

To help you connect with mint as a plant ally, reflect on the following prompts:

How can mint help me clarify and organize the confusion in my life?

_____

_____

_____

What chaos can mint assist me in banishing?

_____

_____

_____

## Elder

I remember the first time I enjoyed elderflower. I was visiting London for the first time and attending a production of *Much Ado About Nothing* at the Globe Theatre. Before the play, we had dinner at the theatre's restaurant. Dessert was an elderflower jelly in a clear glass compote with raspberries suspended in it: beautiful, elegant, and mystical, in its own way. I was charmed by the delicate, subtle flavor—so much so that I still remember it!

Elder is one of the most versatile plants in the realm of herbalism. Its wood is ideal for fashioning wands, instruments, and other tools, its berries are renowned for their healing and immune-boosting properties, and its delicate flowers bring magick and flavor to teas, cocktails, and even desserts. Elder is known for being one of the most magickal trees, sacred to many goddesses and possibly even home to spirits, goddesses, and witches.

**Latin Name:** *Sambucus nigra*

**Folk Names:** Boretree, ellhorn, eldrum

**In Season:** Flowers bloom in early summer, berries ripen in early fall

**Element:** Water

**Ruling Sign:** Libra

**Ruling Planet:** Venus

**Magickal Properties:** Magick, prosperity, luck, protection, healing, banishing, sleep, sacred to witches and goddesses

**Parts of Plant Used:** Flowers, berries, wood

**Magickal Substitutions:** Willow, huckleberry, blackberry

**Other Libra Plants:** Rose, cardamom, lilac, hyacinth

To help you connect with elder as a plant ally, reflect on the following prompts:

What is sacred to the divine feminine within me?

_____

_____

_____

How can elder help me call in prosperity and banish negativity?

_____

_____

_____

## Damiana

Damiana is a powerful herb native to Central and South America and the Caribbean. It has been used for centuries as an aphrodisiac and for sensual and sexual healing of all kinds, bringing it into our awareness as a decidedly witchy and Scorpionic herb. It's a great addition to herbal tea blends for increasing psychic power and lustfulness, as well as for generally supporting intuitive self-love and pleasure.

Scorpio plants tend to be shrouded in mystique and taboo, as most things associated with the sign of the Witch are! Damiana is no different and is a favorite among witches for this reason. Its direct link to taboo subjects like sexuality and psychic visions make it a potent ally for getting in touch with your own intuition and inner darkness.

**Latin Name:** *Turnera diffusa*
**Folk Names:** Old woman's broom, yerba de pastor
**In Season:** Flowers bloom in summer
**Element:** Water
**Ruling Sign:** Scorpio
**Ruling Planet:** Pluto

**Magickal Properties:** Lust, sexuality, love, intuition, psychic visions
**Parts of Plant Used:** Leaves
**Magickal Substitutions:** Patchouli, mugwort, ginseng
**Other Scorpio Plants:** Basil, nettle, pomegranate

To help you connect with damiana as a plant ally, reflect on the following prompts:

What area of my life can damiana help infuse with lustful passion?

_____

_____

_____

How can I embrace my intuition and the personal power it brings me?

_____

_____

_____

## Sage

Sage is one of the most ubiquitous herbs in the spiritual community and has native species pretty much all over the world. However, white sage, which is native to North America, is sacred to indigenous peoples and is currently overharvested. Luckily, all varieties of sage are associated with cleansing and purification so there is no need to use white sage if you do not have indigenous ancestry yourself. It's just as sufficient to burn common garden sage, which is native to Europe. In fact, for those of us descended from European ancestors, it's even more potent to work with a plant connected to our own ancestry as opposed to one taken from other peoples.

The sage plant, the word "sage" (referring to a wise person), and the sign of Sagittarius are all interconnected in the English language. Sagittarius is a passionate, fiery sign dedicated to the learning and dissemination of wisdom. Working with sage as a plant ally can support you in Sagittarian endeavors to cleanse your environment and make space for wisdom.

**Latin Name:** *Salvia officinalis*

**Folk Names:** Common sage, garden sage, sawge

**In Season:** Spring to late fall

**Element:** Air

**Ruling Sign:** Sagittarius

**Ruling Planet:** Jupiter

**Magickal Properties:** Cleansing, wisdom, longevity, wishes, protection

**Parts of Plant Used:** Leaves, oil

**Magickal Substitutions:** Clary sage, any variety of sage, cedar

**Other Sagittarius Plants:** Dandelion, clove, hyssop

To help you connect with sage as a plant ally, reflect on the following prompts:

How can sage help me connect with my deepest inner wisdom?

_____

_____

_____

What needs purifying or cleansing in my life?

_____

_____

_____

## Rosemary

Rosemary is another common kitchen herb that packs a powerful, magickal punch when used with intention and purpose. In Shakespeare's *Hamlet*, Ophelia says, "There's rosemary, that's for remembrance. Pray you, love, remember." The doomed heroine speaks truth, for rosemary is associated with memory, legacy, and honoring the dead.

Rosemary has strong grounding properties that can help you protect your legacy and gain clarity on your memories, perhaps even memories of past lives. It can be burned as a cleansing, purifying herb, much the way that sage commonly is.

**Latin Name:** *Salvia rosmarinus*

**Folk Names:** Elf leaf, compass weed, incensier, dew of the sea

**In Season:** Evergreen

**Element:** Fire

**Ruling Sign:** Capricorn

**Ruling Planet:** Saturn

**Magickal Properties:** Memory, legacy, tradition, protection, purification, clarity, past lives, honoring the dead

**Parts of Plant Used:** Leaves, oil

**Magickal Substitutions:** Sage, cypress, mullein

**Other Capricorn Plants:** Pine, cedar, comfrey

To help you connect with rosemary as a plant ally, reflect on the following prompts:

What do I need to remember about myself, my heritage, or my past lives?

_____

_____

_____

How can rosemary help me protect my legacy?

_____

_____

_____

## Witch Hazel

Witch hazel is an unusual plant (because it flowers in the fall), renowned for its healing properties for centuries. Today, we typically buy it at the drug store in the form of an extract, diluted with alcohol or water. In this form, witch hazel is excellent as a toner and is often used for skin care. Witch hazel is actually a tree native to North America that flowers in the fall and winter when other plants and trees appear dead or in hibernation.

It's fitting that such an unusual plant would be ruled by Aquarius, the Rebel and Revolutionary of the zodiac. Magickally, it is best used for purification so that one can obtain an objective point of view (one of the most cherished qualities of Aquarians). It is also excellent for protection and can aid with intuition as well.

**Latin Name:** _Hamamelis virginiana_
**Folk Names:** Winterbloom
**In Season:** Fall and winter
**Element:** Air
**Ruling Sign:** Aquarius

**Ruling Planet:** Uranus

**Magickal Properties:** Purification, protection, intuition, objective perspectives

**Parts of Plant Used:** Bark, leaves, extract

**Magickal Substitutions:** Sage, rosemary, lavender

**Other Aquarius Plants:** Cacao, air plants, bioluminescent mushrooms

To help you connect with witch hazel as a plant ally, reflect on the following prompts:

Where do I need to acquire a more objective or detached perspective?

_____

_____

_____

What area of my life can witch hazel support me in purifying?

_____

_____

_____

## Mugwort

Mugwort is a favorite herb of many witches, one of the most magickal and mystical of all the plants on this list. Its Latin name references Artemis (the Greek epithet of Diana), the goddess of the hunt, of wildness, animals, and childbirth, who is beloved by many witches.

Mugwort is a highly intuitive herb that can help you connect with your own intuition through psychic visions, dream work, spirit journeys, hedge riding, and astral projection. These are all various ways to receive messages from your intuition, which some believe come from your higher self, others believe come from spirits, and still others believe come from the divine! This is partly because mugwort is considered by many to be a mild psychoactive herb that can induce strange, otherworldly dreams.

**Latin Name:** *Artemisia vulgaris*

**Folk Names:** Wormwood, artemisia, sailor's tobacco, witch herb

**In Season:** Summer and fall

**Element:** Water

**Ruling Sign:** Pisces

**Ruling Planet:** Neptune

**Magickal Properties:** Intuition, psychic visions, dreams, astral protection

**Parts of Plant Used:** Leaves, buds

**Magickal Substitutions:** Lavender, sandalwood, valerian

**Other Pisces Plants:** Bladderwrack, kelp, blueberry

To help you connect with mugwort as a plant ally, reflect on the following prompts:

When I meet mugwort in my dreams, what messages does it share with me?

_____

_____

_____

How can I surrender to trusting my intuition wholly and completely?

_____

_____

_____

## Chapter 2
# CYCLES OF THE MOON

The moon calls so many of us to the path of the witch. All my life, I've pointed up at the sky and exclaimed, "Look at the moon!" no matter what phase it's in. Perhaps you do the same. Our fascination with her phases is innate and primal, something we can't quite explain. Many ancient cultures based their calendars not on the sun but on the moon. In fact, many still do, including the Hebrew, Islamic, and Chinese cultures. Witches flow with the cycles of the moon as a way to understand our moods, emotions, intuition, energy levels, and even to manifest our goals and desires. The moon has many mysteries but also many, many gifts for those willing to listen.

Working with the moon phases is a lesson in patience, magick, and the cyclical nature of the cosmos. In this chapter, we'll explore the four basic moon phases and their energies. There are as many as nine different phases of the moon, depending on whom you ask, but the four basic phases are the most essential.

Each of the four basic phases corresponds to an overarching theme or energy:

- The new moon, which is when the moon is completely dark in the sky, is all about setting intentions, starting new things, and fresh starts.

- The waxing moon, which is when the moon appears to be growing larger and larger, is all about taking action and going after what you want.
- The full moon, which is when the moon is completely illuminated, is all about amplifying your desires, celebrating, and pausing to reflect.
- The waning moon, which is when the moon appears to be growing smaller and smaller, is all about release, letting go, and even banishing what no longer serves you.

As I mentioned in the introduction on page xi, these four phases line up exactly with the energy of the four seasons. The new moon and springtime are for setting intentions. The waxing moon and summer are for taking action. The full moon and autumn are for celebration. And the waning moon and winter are for release. Personally, I don't think this is an accident or coincidence; rather, this is the magick and mystery of nature in motion.

It's helpful to understand the astronomical and astrological cause of each new and full moon in order to understand the energetics. Too often, we rush into the magick and the energetics without understanding the practical, real-world *why* of things! In my experience, the more we understand how nature works, the more magick there is to marvel at.

## THE NEW MOON PHASE

The new moon, when the moon is completely dark in the sky, can only occur when the sun and moon are exactly aligned. The reason that the moon is completely dark from our perspective is not because the moon is not there, but because the side of the moon that we can see from earth is pointing directly away from the sun.

**The only reason the moon appears to be illuminated at all is because the sun is shining on it!** The moon itself does not actually give off light.

In astrology, a new moon occurs when the sun and moon are at the exact same degree of the same sign. Because the sun takes a year to move through all twelve astrological signs and the moon only takes about twenty-eight days to move through all twelve signs, this happens just about once a month. For example, in March or April each year, we have the new moon in Aries, when the sun and moon are both exactly aligned in Aries, the first sign in the zodiac. Then, just about twenty-eight to twenty-nine days later, we have the new moon in Taurus, the second sign in the zodiac, and so on throughout the year.

The new moon is thought to be a new beginning because the moon is dark. It's getting ready to be birthed anew with that first tiny sliver of the crescent moon. It's a time of alignment and power, when the sun and moon are both giving you a boost of energy in the same sign. This period lasts for approximately two and a half days, though the exact new moon happens only briefly. You can take advantage of this new-moon-new-me energy by setting intentions for what you hope and plan to accomplish, receive, or experience in the next moon cycle or over the coming months.

Natural magick is a wonderful tool for helping you clarify and solidify your new moon intentions. Clarity is essential for manifesting your true desires, whether you want love, money, freedom, good health, to hone your psychic ability, or anything else. Clarity and the new moon are both connected to the element of air. You can think of this new moon phase as a gentle breeze that blows the clouds from your mind's eye so that you can clearly visualize what your life will be like once your intentions are realized.

Working with plants that are ruled by the energy of the new moon itself can support you in getting super clear on exactly what it is that you want. Fragrant, purifying herbs like lavender are perfect for embodying this clarifying energy. Then, once you know what you want, it's time to make a clear, solid plan of action to implement during the next moon phase (the waxing moon). I recommend picking just one intention per moon cycle to really go all in with. (Focus also happens to be ruled by the air element!) For example, if you're setting an intention to connect with your intuition, that's still pretty broad. If you aren't sure how to narrow it down, you might sip lavender tea or diffuse peppermint oil while journaling to help you visualize what it would mean for you to connect with your intuition more deeply. What would it feel like to be in tune with your intuition all the time? How would your life be different if that were already true? As you absorb the clarifying wisdom of the plants, maybe you narrow your intention down to drawing a tarot or oracle card every day and journaling on it. This is both a clear intention and an actionable, measurable plan!

## New Moon Correspondences

**Element:** Air

**Related Season:** Spring

**Related Menstrual Phase:** Menstruation

**Goddesses:** Astraea (Greek goddess of innocence and justice), Itzpapalotl (Aztec Obsidian Butterfly goddess)

**Crystals:** Chrysocolla, blue lace agate

**Plants:** Lavender, mint

**Types of Spells or Rituals:** Setting intentions, clarifying desires, calling something new to you such as love or money

## New Moon Diffuser Blend for Clarity

This essential oil blend is perfect for diffusing while you set your new moon intentions each month. These oils are ruled by the element of air and correspond to focus, clarity, and inspiration. They can make you feel emotionally uplifted and mentally energized, as well as bring a bit of mercurial curiosity to your intention-setting practice. Allow yourself to be open and to float from thought to thought and idea to idea as you begin to visualize the possibilities for your future.

- 2 drops clary sage (for wisdom)
- 2 drops grapefruit (for uplifting the spirit)
- 3 drops lavender (for dreaming of possibilities)
- 3 drops lemongrass (for aligning with your intuitive passion)

Place the drops into an ultrasonic diffuser, reed diffuser, or on a salt diffuser (ultrasonic will be the most powerful in diffusing the scent and clarifying properties into your space). Diffuse at your altar or wherever you prefer to sit, visualize, and journal on the future.

How would my life be different than it is now if this intention was already manifested into my life?

_____

_____

_____

What would it feel like to have this thing/experience? (Pro witch tip: Visualize your future self who already lives in this reality and step into their body so that you can truly feel what it's like to have this!)

_____

_____

_____

How can I turn this intention into a more focused and specific plan of action? What's one thing I could accomplish this month to bring my intention into reality?

_____

_____

_____

## THE WAXING MOON PHASE

The waxing moon is the approximately two-week period between the new and full moons, when the moon appears to be growing larger and larger in the sky. As the moon orbits around the earth and the earth orbits around the sun, the portion of the moon that the sun is shining on grows from our perspective on earth. This waxing moon phase can be broken down even further into three smaller phases: the waxing crescent, waxing quarter (also known as the first quarter), and waxing gibbous phases. However, the energy of the waxing moon remains essentially the same throughout these smaller phases, so it is simpler and often more productive to focus on the basics.

The waxing moon is a time of growth and action. This is the period when you're taking action on the intentions you set at the new moon. Natural magick can help you find the stick-with-it-ness within yourself to take practical action on your intentions, but magick is only one component of successful self-care or manifesting. You still need to take the practical actions and do the real-world work in order to bring your desires into existence. It's so easy to set intentions at the new moon and then completely forget about them! That's nothing to be ashamed of or to beat yourself up for—we're all human and sometimes we get distracted by life—but if you have an intention that feels really important to you that you don't want to have fall by the wayside, let your plant allies help!

Creating an herbal talisman to serve as a sensory reminder of your intention is a great way to reinforce it in a practical way. This might be a charm bag, a blessed and magickally dressed candle, or even a small potted plant placed where you'll see it every day. The idea here is to continually be infusing your space and your being with the energy of action. Visual reminders and scent reminders are both powerful ways of instilling the action in you and making it habitual.

Although you can hold rituals to honor all four phases of the moon, I typically find that the waxing moon is better suited to taking action than to reflecting or performing rituals. Though, if you were to do a waxing moon ritual, the first quarter moon would be ideal, as the peak of waxing energy is about halfway between the new and full moons.

## Waxing Moon Correspondences

**Element:** Fire

**Related Season:** Summer

**Related Menstrual Phase:** Follicular

**Goddesses:** Athena (Greek goddess of wisdom and war), Freya (Norse goddess of love and war)

**Crystals:** Carnelian, citrine

**Plants:** Calendula, cinnamon

**Types of Spells or Rituals:** Supporting your practical actions, giving your actions and intentions a boost of power

## Waxing Moon Charm Bag for Taking Action

Charm bags are one of my absolute favorite types of spells, as they are so easy, accessible, and effective. A charm bag is a small bag filled with plants, crystals, or other items that is charged with a specific purpose. In this case, you're creating a charm bag to serve as a visual reminder of your new moon intentions to inspire you to take action. It also happens to smell wonderful!

- Small muslin or taffeta bag or sachet
- 1 fresh sprig or 1 tablespoon dried goldenseal (for manifestation)
- 1 orange peel (for prosperity)
- 1 whole cinnamon stick (for power and success)
- Small citrine crystal (for success)

Place each ingredient in the bag carefully and reverently, focusing on your intention and the specific actions you plan to take to bring it into reality. Tie the bag shut and place it somewhere you'll see every day (perhaps multiple times a day), such as in the center console of your car, next to your computer or desk, or in your purse or bag.

## THE FULL MOON PHASE

The full moon is the most magickal, witchy, and intuitive phase. Something about the pull of the full moon brings out our inner wildness. Emergency operators and hospitals often report an increase in chaos and emotional incidents at the full moon. Women accused of witchcraft during the witch trial periods in Europe were often accused of cavorting with demons under a full moon, and the goddess Diana, who is often worshipped by modern witches, is associated with the moon.

A full moon can only occur when the sun is shining on the entire side of the moon that faces the earth. Astrologically, this can only happen when the sun and moon are in exact opposition to one another (lined up across the sky exactly in opposite zodiac signs). For example, during Aries season, the sun is in Aries and the full moon is in Libra, because Aries and Libra are opposites. I like to call this the "white dot in the black sea" because the full moon is like a little dose of the opposite energy of the current season. We are collectively drawn to certain actions, themes, and ideals during each astrological season (the period the sun spends in each sign). The new moon reinforces the energy of that season, while the full moon brings us balance and perspective by asking us to experience the opposite energy for a few days and to pause to celebrate it.

Releasing rituals are very popular and common during this phase, but there is an important nuance here: at the full moon, you're releasing control and expectations so that the universe can co-create something amazing with you, as opposed to releasing or letting go of things you don't want. The full moon is like the moment you take your foot off the gas ahead of an approaching stop sign but before you start braking and actively slowing down. We have the entire two-week period of the waning moon to work on actively releasing and letting go!

In fact, the full moon serves an important and very often overlooked role in the self-care and manifestation cycles. When you're trying to bring a desire into existence, it's important to set a clear intention, yes, and to take practical, aligned action.

The full moon represents what is often the missing piece of this manifestation puzzle: celebration, reflection, and gratitude. If you don't take the time to reflect on what's worked so far and what hasn't, so that you can adjust course if necessary or express gratitude for how far you've come (even if you haven't quite reached your goal yet), you're likely to find yourself in a constant cycle of burnout. That's why celebration, gratitude, and reflection at the full moon are one of the most important aspects of the moon cycle overall.

Natural magick can help you tune into this intuitive and celebratory energy by calming your nervous system and encouraging you to take time for meditation and reflection. There are lots of plants ruled by the element of water and by the moon itself, which are ideal for the full moon phase when the moon is at the peak of its intuitive (and gravitational) power. Soothing, relaxing ways to work with your plant allies during this phase include drinking tea, anointing with calming oils, and even meditating on or meeting a moon-ruled plant in a spirit journey.

## Full Moon Correspondences

**Element:** Water

**Related Season:** Autumn

**Related Menstrual Phase:** Ovulation

**Goddesses:** Diana (Roman goddess of the moon and the hunt), Changxi (Chinese goddess of the moon)

**Crystals:** Moonstone, labradorite

**Plants:** Jasmine, eucalyptus

**Types of Spells or Rituals:** Amplification of love or gratitude, connecting with intuition and spirit

## Full Moon Tea for Reflection

This tea blend is one of the very first that I ever made for myself and one of my first forays into the world of natural magick! It remains one of my favorites and I look forward to sipping this delicious tea every full moon.

This blend contains plants ruled by the element of water and that are connected to intuition. The flavor is floral forward with hints of warm spice and gentle, soothing energy. It's perfect for sipping while watching the moonrise, in a ritual bath, or just aligning with the grateful, loving energy of the full moon throughout your day.

- 3 parts white peony tea leaves (for intuition)
- 1 part rosebuds (for gratitude)
- 1 part jasmine flowers (for intuition)
- ½ part green cardamom pods (for love)

Gently crush the cardamom pods with a mortar and pestle or the back of a wooden spoon. Combine the ingredients in a small bowl, then scoop into a tea infuser or empty tea bag. Place the infuser or tea bag in a cup and pour hot water over it. Allow to steep for 3 to 5 minutes, then remove infuser or tea bag.

## THE WANING MOON PHASE

Finally, the waning moon, the approximately two-week period between the full and new moons, is when the moon appears to be getting smaller and smaller in the sky. Like the waxing moon, we can break this phase down into smaller phases (four, this time!). The waning moon consists of the waning gibbous phase, the waning (or last) quarter phase, the waning crescent phase, and the dark moon.

The definition of the dark moon is a hotly debated topic in the witchy and spiritual communities, as there are a few different definitions which all make sense in their own way. I work with the dark moon as the last day or two before the new moon (the portion of the waning phase when the moon is almost completely dark in the sky) and consider it to be our last opportunity to release what no longer serves us before setting intentions on the new moon (when the sun and moon are exactly aligned). This is the definition we are working with in this book. However, some witches consider the dark moon as the phase when the moon is completely dark in the sky, and the new moon as the first sliver of the crescent moon. You should go with whatever definition resonates most with you.

The waning moon is a period of release, letting go, and even banishing what no longer serves us. This is the time to reflect on what actions, thoughts, patterns, or beliefs have not served you in the past few weeks since you set your new moon intentions and to let them go (or at least to work on letting them go, since release is not always something that comes easily or immediately).

Releasing is one of those spiritual terms that we throw around a lot but isn't always explained very well. For many of us, it's not in our nature to easily let go of something we once valued or felt a sense of control over. It's one thing to say you're releasing the shadows and bad habits that have held you back . . . and another to let them go truly, fully from your life. If you've ever felt resistant to releasing, natural magick can be a beautiful tool for creating a gentler, more supported way to do so.

Our plant allies are not obsessed with control in the same way that we humans are. Plants move through the cycles of the moon and the seasons without complaint or frustration that they are in any one phase or another. They also do not resist the hibernation period that winter brings, the season that is energetically aligned with the waning moon. This is a lovely lesson just to meditate on, but you can also channel the magick of certain plants with releasing energy to support you during this phase.

## Waning Moon Correspondences

**Element:** Earth

**Related Season:** Winter

**Related Menstrual Phase:** Luteal

**Goddesses:** Hekate (Greek goddess of witchcraft), Persephone (Greek goddess of vegetation and the underworld)

**Crystals:** Smoky quartz, fluorite

**Plants:** Dandelion root, mugwort

**Types of Spells or Rituals:** Banishing, releasing, cutting ties with people or ideas that no longer serve you

## Waning Moon Bath Salts for Banishing Negativity

Ritual baths are excellent for celebrating any of the four moon phases, but I find that I crave them most during the waning moon. Collectively, we tend to be a bit more tired or need extra nourishment and support during the waning moon, so ritual baths can be deeply soothing at this time. They're also the perfect opportunity for a little cleansing and banishing spell to rid yourself of any negative energies you've picked up through your day or over the past moon cycle. Adding infused salts or oils to your bath is a great way to bring natural magick into your ritual. This bath salt blend is designed to help you relax and retreat, then release any heaviness that has been weighing on you.

- 2 cups Epsom salts
- ⅓ cup baking soda
- ¼ cup dried elderflowers (for protection from negative energy)
- ¼ cup dried lavender flowers (for relaxation and soothing)
- 10–15 drops sandalwood oil (for banishing negativity)
- 5–10 drops vetiver oil (for breaking through blocks)

Mix the salts, baking soda, and dried flowers together in a bowl so that they are evenly combined. Add the drops of essential oils and mix thoroughly to combine. Scoop into a jar and store in a cool, dry place. Allow to infuse for at least a week before use. If you'd like to make this recipe right away and add the ingredients directly to your bath without prior infusion, use no more than 6 to 8 drops of essential oils total as more than this can be too intense for direct contact with skin.

Add the infused salts to your warm bath water. You might also accompany your bath with some banishing crystals like black tourmaline or obsidian, black candles, and a soothing cup of tea. Allow yourself to fully and deeply relax as much as possible.

When you feel complete, rise from the bath and rinse the water and salts from your skin. Step out of the bath and release the drain. Remain sitting or standing beside the tub for the entire duration as the water drains. Watch the water disappear from view and imagining any heaviness, doubt, fear, shame, or other troubling feelings or experiences

you've had recently draining along with it. When the water has completely drained, there will be salt and flowers on the bottom of the tub; take this opportunity to rinse them down the drain, banishing the last of what no longer serves you this month.

## WORKING WITH THE MOON (AND WHY YOU SHOULD)

In astrology and witchcraft, we talk a lot about "working with" the energy of the seasons, moon phases, planets, goddesses, crystals, and plants, but what does that really mean? Working with the energy of something is about opening yourself up to its wisdom and allowing yourself to be guided, rather than trying to lead the way yourself. It's a process of cocreation, of allowing yourself to be influenced by the wisdom of nature, while simultaneously grounding that wisdom in the practical, mundane realities of life.

There are many layers of working with the moon, varying in their degree of depth and commitment. I always recommend moonbathing: simply spending time outside in the moonlight or even just looking up at the moon through the window. The more you do this, the more aware you'll become of where and when the moon rises near your home, its current phase, and its influence on you personally. Awareness is one of the witch's greatest tools.

However, I believe the single most powerful way to work with the moon is tracking your moods, energy levels, dreams, and menstrual cycle (if you have one), by the moon phases and signs. This doesn't need to be an overwhelming or daunting endeavor at all. In fact, you can do it with little more than a smartphone and your notes app or a journal! Luckily, there are tons of great moon phase and moon calendar apps for both Android and Apple that make this really easy, including iLuna and The Moon Calendar by Laura Haworth. Tracking with the moon phases and signs will help you become more aware of not only what the moon is up to but how its subtle, energetic, cosmic shifts can impact you in personal and profound ways.

Here's what you do:

1. Download an app that appeals to you, preferably one that shows you both the current moon phase and the moon sign.
2. Each morning when you wake up, check this app and make a note of what the current phase and sign are. Then, take a few notes about how you're feeling, what your energy level and mood are

like, and maybe write down your dreams or record where you are in your menstrual cycle, especially if you have a natural, non-hormone regulated cycle. (Don't worry if this doesn't apply to you. It doesn't apply to me either, but I know it's profound for some people!)

3. You might also incorporate this into a larger morning ritual by drawing a tarot or oracle card, lighting some candles, and doing meditation or yoga, but checking the moon phase and sign can stand alone as a ritual itself. Spend as little or as much time on this as you feel called to.

4. Track this every day (or every few days) for at least one to two months. Then, take some time, especially at a full moon, to reflect back on your notes and notice the patterns that start to emerge. During which moon phases do you feel most energetic or inspired? Which moon signs are your lowest energy days when you need more rest or alone time? This information about yourself can be invaluable for not only creating the life you want but also being more in flow with nature and your own unique rhythms.

5. You can take this one step further by also tracking where each moon sign activates in your own chart! Generate your astrological natal chart from one of the many free sites online, such as www.astro.com or www.astro-charts.com, and change the settings to "Whole Signs Houses," which will place one sign in each house in your chart. Note the house and any planets that are activated for you by each moon sign for even deeper and more personal insight.

Other methods for working with the moon include:

- Meditate while holding moon crystals such as moonstone, selenite, labradorite, or amethyst.
- Create an altar and pray or journey with a moon goddess such as Artemis/Diana (Greek/Roman), Changxi (Chinese), Selene/Luna (Greek/Roman), Hekate (Greek), or Mama Quilla (Incan).
- Drink moon teas or diffuse essential oils made with plants such as jasmine, white peony, or rose.
- Hold new moon rituals to activate your new intentions.
- Hold full moon rituals to reflect and celebrate.
- Hold waxing and waning quarter moon rituals to check in with your intentions and reflect.

The moon's ever-shifting cycles impact us so much more than we realize in our technology-focused lives. Even just bringing more awareness to the moon can be life altering, let alone intentionally opening yourself up to her wisdom through ritual, reflection, and energy-directing tools.

## LUNAR ASTROLOGY

As the moon moves through the twelve signs of the zodiac, we experience a new moon in every sign and a full moon in every sign (sometimes two) throughout the year. In the seasonal chapters later in this book, I'll be sharing journal prompts and herbal recipes for working with each of the new and full moons through the seasons.

However, these new and full moons (and the transits of the moon throughout the month, regardless of phase) also activate particular areas of your own astrological chart. We haven't talked much about your astrological chart yet, but lunar astrology is the perfect way to get started! As the moon moves around the sky, it also moves around your own natal chart.

Your natal chart (also known as your astrological chart or your birth chart) is a map of the planets at the moment you were born. There are lots of great websites where you can generate your natal chart for free, including my own: www.witchoflupinehollow.com/create-your-birth-chart. I highly recommend changing your settings on whatever site you choose to show "Whole Signs Houses." There are many different house systems, and all are valid, but Whole Signs Houses is the oldest and simplest.

**You will need your birth date, birth location, and exact birth time to generate a completely accurate chart.** If you don't know your exact birth time, you can still generate a chart without houses or an ascendant. Bear in mind that your moon sign may or may not be accurate if you do this, but the sun and the rest of the planets will be.

Your chart is divided into the twelve signs and then into the twelve houses. Each house is naturally ruled by a particular sign, so the energy of that sign and that house are aligned. Unless you have Aries rising, you will have a different sign in each house than the sign that naturally rules it. You have one sign in every house, and you may or may not have planets, the sun and moon (called luminaries), or asteroids in all of them.

As the moon moves through the twelve signs, spending just about 2.5 days in each one, it also moves through those twelve signs and twelve houses in your own chart. This activates the energy of each house as well as the energy of any planets, luminaries, or asteroids that you have in that house.

For example, I have my sun in Taurus in the 9th house. Therefore, every month, when the moon is in Taurus, it is activating my sun and the energy of both Taurus and the 9th house for me. Although there are twelve signs, twelve houses, two luminaries, eight planets, and tons of asteroids and other celestial bodies, understanding your astrological chart and all the different energies and themes present in it is actually quite a bit simpler than it might seem. See, every planet naturally rules a particular sign, and every sign naturally rules a particular house, so rather than being separate entities, it's more like each planet, sign, and house are a group of entities that all represent a similar or related energy.

Here are a few reference charts to understand the energy of each sign, house, and planet at a glance:

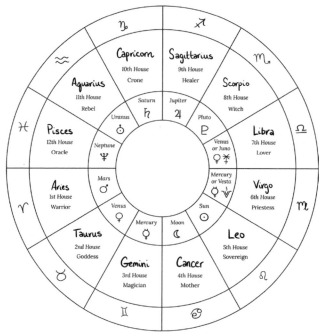

*Designed by Angela Pustorino*

| Sign & House | Energy |
|---|---|
| Aries (ruled by Mars) & 1st house | Self, action, passion |
| Taurus (ruled by Venus) & 2nd house | Pleasure, ease, simplicity |
| Gemini (ruled by Mercury) & 3rd house | Curiosity, communication, social |
| Cancer (ruled by the moon) & 4th house | Self-care, home, intuition |
| Leo (ruled by the sun) & 5th house | Joy, fun, play |
| Virgo (ruled by Mercury and asteroid, Vesta) & 6th house | Ritual, routine, wellness |
| Libra (ruled by Venus and asteroid, Juno) & 7th house | Relationships, fairness, balance |
| Scorpio (ruled by Pluto) & 8th house | Depth, magick, shadows |
| Sagittarius (ruled by Jupiter) & 9th house | Exploration, adventure, wisdom |
| Capricorn (ruled by Saturn) & 10th house | Ambition, structure, accountability |
| Aquarius (ruled by Uranus) & 11th house | Revolution, community, social justice |
| Pisces (ruled by Neptune) & 12th house | Transcendence, spirituality, release |

| Planet/Luminary/Asteroid | Energy |
|---|---|
| Sun | Joy, happiness, light |
| Moon | Emotions, intuition |
| Mercury | Communication, curiosity |
| Venus | Love, desires, beauty |
| Mars | Action, anger, passion |
| Jupiter | Expansion, luck, spirituality |
| Saturn | Restriction, responsibilities |
| Uranus | Revolution, change |
| Neptune | Dreams, illusion, confusion |
| Pluto | Transformation, destruction |
| Ceres (Asteroid) | Self-care, nurturing |
| Vesta (Asteroid) | Ritual, sacred sexuality |
| Pallas (Asteroid) | Manifestation |
| Juno (Asteroid) | Sacred union, relationships |
| Black Moon Lilith (lunar apogee) | Inner darkness, impulses, sexuality |
| Chiron (actually a centaur, not an asteroid) | The Wounded Healer (your core wound but also your greatest healing gift) |

Let's do a fun exercise to help you understand what is being activated for you each month as the moon moves around your chart. In the following table, write down each of your house signs in the second column, then note if you have any planets in that house in the third column. Finally, write down the combined energy of the house, sign, and planets (if any), in the fourth column, based on the tables above.

| Sign | House | Planets | Combined Energy (House & Sign Energy + Planet/Luminary/ Asteroid Energy, if any) |
|------|-------|---------|------------------------------------------------------------------|
| Ex. Taurus | Ex. Ninth | Ex. Sun | Ex. Pleasure, ease, simplicity/exploration, adventure, wisdom/joy, happiness, light |
| | First | | |
| | Second | | |
| | Third | | |
| | Fourth | | |
| | Fifth | | |
| | Sixth | | |
| | Seventh | | |
| | Eighth | | |
| | Ninth | | |
| | Tenth | | |
| | Eleventh | | |
| | Twelfth | | |

Now you can see that as the moon moves through the twelve signs, it's activating specific energies in your own chart! When it meets up with the sun, moon, and other planets in your chart, those are likely to be particularly potent and active (or potentially tiring) days for you. When a new or full moon activates a busy area of your chart, those days will be especially potent. In fact, all of the planets activate each house and sign in your chart as they move, though much more slowly than the moon does! This is powerful information to have as you begin to deepen your natural magick practice. I encourage you to refer back to this chart often as you move through the seasons and the new and full moons throughout the year, to be mindful of your own energy and what is currently being activated for you.

For example, an Aries new moon is traditionally and collectively a time of great passion, action, and forward movement. However, if Aries activates your moon or Neptune, or your 4th, 8th, or 12th houses, it might be a more restful, introverted, and intuitive time for you, though the generally active energy of Aries will still be present. You can start creating your own natural magick recipes and spells that channel not only the collective energy of the season or moon phase, but also the energy of your own unique chart. Working with the moon phases and astrology in this deeply personal way can lend much greater nuance and customization to your natural magick practice.

# Chapter 3
# CYCLES OF THE SUN

In the twenty-first century, we have become increasingly disconnected from the sun's presence. Only a few generations ago, our ancestors literally *lived* by the light of the sun. Especially in agricultural communities, they rose with sunrise and slept with sunset or shortly after. But as electricity moved into the streets and eventually into our homes, we became free to sleep and wake when we chose. I, for one, am immensely grateful for this freedom, yet it has its downsides too. When it starts to get dark earlier and earlier in the late fall and winter months, instead of being in flow with the energy of rest and introspection, we just flip on a light and keep right on working. We barely notice the subtle shifts around the solstices and equinoxes, when the sun's power is most highlighted, because we aren't as in tune with that power anymore.

By contrast, our ancestors were so deeply in tune with the sun that they built monuments to align with these solar events: Stonehenge, Machu Picchu, the Easter Island Moai, and so many more scattered across the globe. This wasn't merely cosmic fascination; the solstices and equinoxes marked important shifts in the sun's power that impacted our ancestors' survival in very real and tangible ways. In ancient times, and really not so very long ago, life was a cycle of planting and tending

crops through spring and summer with the hope that there would be an abundant harvest in the fall to feed everyone through the winter (because if there were *not* abundant crops to feed them through the winter, the consequences could be dire).

Between electricity, imported foods, and greenhouse tomatoes, we barely even have to know what time of year it is, let alone worry if the crops will be abundant enough to feed us through the winter. Greenhouses, electricity, and all our other modern innovations are not to be taken for granted; they make survival less of an immediate, ever-present concern. But they don't necessarily help us thrive, either. Luckily, we don't have to move off the grid to reclaim our connection to the sun!

Working with the cycles of the sun is a practice in mindfulness and being present, of bringing our awareness to the quiet, subtle shifts in the weather and the light. It's also a practice of being in tune with the ebb and flow of energy throughout the year. We tend to think of the seasons as an expression of the earth, but they are really an expression of the sun's effect on the earth. Depending on the strength of the sun, the earth and plants and even animals respond in corresponding ways.

We are not meant to hustle and produce and be energetic every day of the year—or even every month. This becomes very obvious when we look to nature. As the sun's power dips and wanes in fall and into winter, the plants reserve their energy in their roots, resting and waiting to return in spring. Animals hibernate or become less active, relying on the stores of food they've squirreled away in the warmer months. The natural cycle of both the earth and the sun moves from this restful, hibernating state of winter, when the sun is at its lowest point in the sky and daylight hours are at their shortest, into the hopefulness of springtime. In late winter and early spring, the days begin to grow longer and the sun grows stronger, reaching a point of balance at the equinox when daylight and nighttime hours are equal. Over the spring and early summer months, the sun grows to its full strength up to the summer solstice, the longest day of the year. As we slowly wind down into autumn, the sun's power wanes once more, reaching a point of balance at the autumn equinox, then finally the lowest point once more at the winter solstice. We give gratitude for the harvest of abundance and life-sustaining plants in autumn that will carry us through the darkest nights of winter.

Being in flow with the cycles of the sun means honoring these natural rhythms with intention. It means breaking out of the hyperproductive spin cycle of our society and returning our attention to the cycle of life and death that our ancestors lived by. This might sound disconnected from your real, daily life—or even a little macabre—but what if we see it as the cycle of life, from seed to growth to harvest to death? You can apply this same cycle to so many different areas of life. The seed phase is when we make plans, the growth phase is when we take action, the harvest phase is when we pause to celebrate, and the death phase is when we rest and retreat.

This natural rhythm is pretty much universal—it's the energy of the four seasons, the energy of the four moon phases, and the energy of life. And each phase of the cycle is just as important as the other three. If you are missing even just one, you're missing an essential step in nurturing yourself and creating the life you desire. We don't get to just skip over winter or the waning moon, so how can we expect to skip over the literal and metaphorical death or rest phases of life ? Death and rest are not macabre or a waste of time that could be used more productively; rather, they help us to recover, reflect, and prepare for what's to come.

When you flow through the natural cycles of life, you're setting yourself up for success. That might be financial success, success in your career or a project, or simply pleasure and enjoyment. Or it might be success in the form of feeling nourished, fulfilled, and in tune with the needs of your mind, body, and intuition. (Even better, it might be success in *all* of these areas!) Working with these cycles can have very tangible results.

## Seed (Plan)

The seed phase is springtime, when our ancestors were planting and when we make plans. This is when the flowers start to bloom again, the grass gets greener, birds return from the south, and baby animals are born. We associate spring with fresh, energizing plants, flowers, and

scents. Energetically, this time of year is about fresh starts and new beginnings.

Plants that are in season in springtime include daffodils, tulips, lilacs, and spring greens like green onions, kale, and chard. Citrus fruits are starting to wind down from their peak in late winter and we might start to see the very beginning of summer flowers like roses and lavender.

## Growth (Act)

The growth phase is summertime, when crops grow abundantly and we take action. Summer is the long stretch of warm days when flowers and vegetables are both in abundance, gardens are overflowing, and there are so many things to see and do. Energetically, this time of year is about taking action and putting your plans in motion. Plants that are in season include roses, jasmine, lavender, almost all fresh herbs such as mint, thyme, oregano, and basil, and summer vegetables like tomatoes and zucchini. We also see lots of berries this time of year, including blueberries, strawberries, raspberries, and blackberries.

## Harvest (Gratitude)

The harvest phase is autumn, when our ancestors harvested crops and we harvest the outcomes of our manifestations. This is when stores are filled with all the delicious, spiced flavors of fall. Brilliantly colored leaves fall gently to the ground and magick is in the air. Energetically, this time of year is about celebration and gratitude. It's an opportunity to pause to reflect and be grateful for all the abundance that has come our way in the previous seasons. Plants that are in season include pumpkins, apples, pears, and pomegranates. We also see lots of squash and gourds like acorn squash and butternut squash and fall flowers like chrysanthemums. Many herbs still grow abundantly until the first frost as well.

## Death (Rest)

The death phase is winter, when the earth hibernates and we reach a much-needed period of rest. This is when the earth turns within and plants and animals alike save their energy. We have a tendency to want to skip this phase, but it is oh-so-important to rest before we begin again in the spring. Energetically, this time of year is about retreat and reflection, taking time to refuel our minds and bodies. It's an opportunity to take stock and decide what aspects of ourselves from the past year are coming with us into the new one—and which we're leaving behind. Although most plants don't grow in winter, there are a few in season including citrus, like lemons, limes, oranges, grapefruits, kumquats, and bergamot. Winter vegetables like beets and kale are prevalent as well, and we see certain flowers such as snowdrops, especially toward the end of the season. And, of course, the evergreen trees are still standing stalwart, which is why we bring their branches into our homes this time of year to celebrate the inevitable return of the light and of life.

There are many ways you can work with the different energies of the four seasons. Cooking and working with seasonal plants are some of my favorite ways, which is exactly what we'll be exploring later in this book! There are two basic components of the seasons that can help you stay accountable to your goal of being in tune with the seasonal energies: the twelve astrological signs and the eight pagan sabbats, or holidays. In the rest of this chapter, I'm going to share an overview of these two components. Understanding these two interlocking cycles of the sun is very important, as they help us mark the passage of the entire year.

## THE TWELVE ASTROLOGICAL SIGNS

From our perspective on earth, the sun appears to move through the twelve constellations, or signs, of the zodiac every year, spending just about one month in each sign. It spends the same month (give or take a day or two) in each sign every year. We call these astrological seasons, like Aries season or Cancer season.

This means that the sun is moving through, or transiting, particular signs during each season:

- In spring, the sun is in Aries, Taurus, and Gemini
- In summer, the sun is in Cancer, Leo, and Virgo
- In autumn, the sun is in Libra, Scorpio, and Sagittarius
- In winter, the sun is in Capricorn, Aquarius, and Pisces

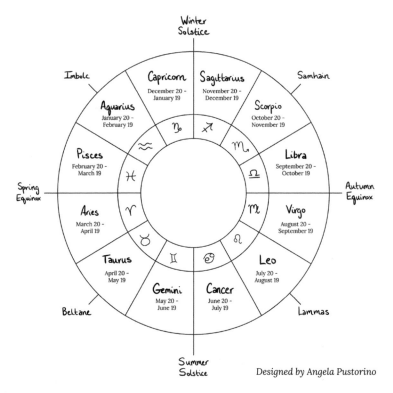

Winter Solstice

Imbolc

Capricorn
December 20 –
January 19

Sagittarius
November 20 –
December 19

Samhain

Aquarius
January 20 –
February 19

Scorpio
October 20 –
November 19

Pisces
February 20 –
March 19

Libra
September 20 –
October 19

Spring Equinox

Autumn Equinox

Aries
March 20 –
April 19

Virgo
August 20 –
September 19

Taurus
April 20 –
May 19

Leo
July 20 –
August 19

Beltane

Gemini
May 20 –
June 19

Cancer
June 20 –
July 19

Lammas

Summer Solstice

*Designed by Angela Pustorino*

This probably makes sense since you likely know your sun sign off the top of your head and will notice that it aligns with the season you were born in. (These are reversed in the Southern Hemisphere, with autumn starting at Aries season, winter starting at Cancer season, spring starting at Libra season, and summer starting at Capricorn season.)

But let's take it a step further. The movement of the sun through the twelve signs is not coincidentally connected to the seasons. It actually triggers them! Each sign is divided into 30°, so the sun moves at a rate of approximately one degree per day. When the sun reaches 0° of the first sign in each season, called the cardinal sign, this is what triggers the solstices and equinoxes.

- The spring equinox occurs when the sun reaches 0° Aries.
- The summer solstice occurs when the sun reaches 0° Cancer.
- The autumn equinox occurs when the sun reaches 0° Libra.
- The winter solstice occurs when the sun reaches 0° Capricorn.

The energy of these four cardinal signs is all about starting new things. They are the initiators of the zodiac, who go out and get things *done*. Each sign also has a natural opposite, which is reflected in the cardinal signs. Aries and Libra (initiators of the two equinoxes) are opposites and Cancer and Capricorn (initiators of the two solstices) are opposites.

The middle sign of each season (Taurus, Leo, Scorpio, and Aquarius) is what's called a fixed sign, and these are the signs that carry us through the longest stretch of each season. The energy of fixed signs is all about sustaining projects and ideas and sustaining us through the height of each season.

The last sign of each season (Gemini, Virgo, Sagittarius, and Pisces) is what's called a mutable sign, and these are the signs that lead us through the transition from one season to the next. The energy of mutable signs is all about being changeable and adaptable—like adapting from the energy of one season and shifting into the next one!

We can work with herbalism to embody not only the energy of the current season, but also the energy of the current sign within each season. Every sign is associated with certain symbols, archetypes, colors, goddesses, plants, crystals, and more. As discussed in Chapter 1, these associated materials are called magickal correspondences because they correspond to and help us channel the energy of each sign. See Chapters 5–8 to discover magickal correspondences for each sign and season.

# THE WHEEL OF THE YEAR

As the sun transits each of the twelve signs of the zodiac, of course, we also experience the four seasons: spring, summer, autumn, and winter. Many pagans and witches mark the passing of the seasons with the eight sabbats, sacred holidays and festivals, which altogether form the Wheel of the Year. This idea of the Wheel of the Year reinforces the cyclical nature of the seasons and of life, as it is an ever-continuing wheel of celebrations without a true beginning or end.

Four of the eight sabbats are the solstices and equinoxes, the astronomical and astrological start of each new season. The spring and autumn equinoxes are days of balance when daylight and nighttime hours are equal. The summer and winter solstices are days of extremes. The summer solstice is the longest day of the year, when the sun is at its peak, or *zenith*, while the winter solstice is the longest night of the year, when the sun is at its lowest point, or *nadir*. Each has many names, though the most commonly known now were assigned in modern times and are not really rooted in ancient traditions.

**It's important to note that the eight sabbats were not celebrated altogether anywhere in the ancient world.** Rather, each sabbat has been individually celebrated in a variety of regions across Europe with similar themes and ideas found in cultures around the world.

The other four festivals of the Wheel of the Year are referred to as "fire festivals" (as they are often celebrated with candles, flame, and bonfires) or "cross-quarter days" (as they divide each season, or quarter of the year, in half). Each season contains one fire festival, which always occurs when the sun is in the fixed signs of the zodiac. The spring and fall fire festivals of Beltane and Samhain occur in Taurus and Scorpio seasons, which are opposites, while the summer and winter fire festivals of Lammas and Imbolc occur in Leo and Aquarius seasons, which are also opposites. These festivals occur on the thirty-first or first of the month, just about halfway between the nearest solstice and equinox. There are no sabbats that occur during the mutable signs, which lead right up to the moment of the equinox or solstice in the sign and season that follow them.

Some witches choose to celebrate the fire festivals on astrological or lunar dates, as opposed to calendar dates. Astrologically, they would be celebrated when the sun reaches 15° of their sign, which is the midpoint of each astrological season and the exact halfway point between the equinox and solstice on either side. Lunar dates for the fire festivals are celebrated on the nearest full moon in the opposite sign. I've noted the astrological and lunar dates for the fire festivals in the following sections along with the calendar dates. All of these celebration dates are valid and it's best to celebrate on whichever dates resonate most with you. I like to think of the sabbats as a season unto themselves, a portion of the larger four seasons of the year that brings with it a particular perspective and nuance.

## Spring Equinox

The spring equinox is sometimes called Ostara, named for the Gaulish goddess of springtime, though this is a modern construction. The equinox takes place when the sun moves into Aries and is a celebration of new beginnings and the astrological new year. Some common celebrations include dyeing hard-boiled eggs with natural dyes made from plants like cabbage, berries, and coffee, as well as other symbols of fertility like bunnies and baby animals. (Many of the symbols and celebrations of the spring equinox may be familiar to you as symbols of secular Easter. That's because modern Easter traditions were co-opted from pagan celebrations of the equinox. In fact, the date of Easter is actually calculated based on the first full moon after the equinox itself which is why it changes from year to year.) It's also common to eat fresh, seasonal, springtime veggies and herbs at the equinox, such as asparagus, Swiss chard, and dill.

One of the most important rituals at the spring equinox is setting "new year" intentions for the rest of the year. That's because the spring equinox always occurs on the first day of Aries season, the first sign in the zodiac, and is also known as the astrological new year. Refer to page 90 to learn more about the correspondences of Aries for the spring equinox as well.

- **Calendar Date:** Approximately March 20 (can shift up to 3 days in either direction)
- **Astrological Date:** When the sun reaches 0° Aries
- **Lunar Date:** Not applicable
- **Astrological Season:** Aries
- **Alternate Names:** Ostara, Eostre, astrological new year
- **Goddesses:** Ostara (Gaulish goddess of spring), Flora (Roman goddess of spring)
- **Crystals:** Peridot, aventurine
- **Plants:** Lavender, lemon

*Note: The above information is for the Northern Hemisphere. In the Southern Hemisphere, the autumn equinox occurs when the sun reaches 0° Aries around March 20. Refer to the Libra season and autumn equinox sections for correspondences.*

## Beltane

The spring fire festival is Beltane, which takes place May 1 during Taurus season and is a celebration of life and fertility. The name Beltane is widely known as a combination of two Celtic words relating to fire, "bel" and "teine." One of the most common and visible symbols of Beltane is the Maypole dance, from Germanic and Celtic regions, that involves intertwining colorful ribbons around a standing pole. Traditional Beltane rituals include practicing magick and divination and celebrating fertility and sexuality. It's also common to make offerings to the fae at Beltane, though it's a good idea to really do your research before opening a relationship with these sometimes volatile or unpredictable energies. Refer to page 100 to learn more about the correspondences of Taurus for Beltane as well.

- **Calendar Date:** May 1
- **Astrological Date:** When sun reaches midpoint of Taurus season (15° Taurus)
- **Lunar Date:** Full moon in Scorpio (could occur anytime between April 20–May 20)
- **Astrological Season:** Taurus
- **Alternate Names:** Bealtaine, Beltany, May Day, Walpurgis Night
- **Goddesses:** Persephone (Greek goddess of vegetation and the underworld), Venus (Roman goddess of love)
- **Crystals:** Rose quartz, rhodochrosite
- **Plants:** Rose, hawthorn

*Note: The above information is for the Northern Hemisphere. In the Southern Hemisphere, the festival of Samhain occurs during Taurus season in May. Refer to the Scorpio season and Samhain sections for correspondences.*

## Summer Solstice

The summer solstice is sometimes called Litha, which originates as the Anglo-Saxon name for the months of June and July. The solstice takes place when the sun moves into Cancer and is a celebration of light, sunshine, and abundance, as this is the longest day of the year with the most daylight hours. There's a "lazy, hazy days of summer" vibe about the solstice and it is truly about relaxation, fun, and joyfulness.

Eating seasonal summer fruits and veggies is a good way to celebrate, but so is a good old-fashioned backyard barbecue or beach day. Spending lots of time outside in the sunshine on the solstice is ideal. One of the most important traditions for the summer solstice is to watch the sunrise and/or sunset and really soak up the rays of the sun. In recent years, Stonehenge and other locations have begun livestreaming sunrise and sunset so that pagans around the world can tune in for a truly ancient or ancestral experience. Refer to page 128 to learn more about the correspondences of Cancer for the summer solstice as well.

- **Calendar Date:** Approximately June 20 (can shift up to 3 days in either direction)
- **Astrological Date:** When the sun reaches 0° Cancer
- **Lunar Date:** Not applicable
- **Astrological Season:** Cancer
- **Alternate Names:** Litha, midsummer
- **Goddesses:** Áine (Irish goddess of summer), Amaterasu (Japanese sun goddess)
- **Crystals:** Sunstone, citrine
- **Plants:** Sunflower, oak

Note: *The above information is for the Northern Hemisphere. In the Southern Hemisphere, the winter solstice occurs when the sun reaches 0° Cancer around June 20. Refer to the Capricorn season and winter solstice sections for correspondences.*

## Lammas

The summer fire festival is Lammas, also known as Lughnasadh, which takes place August 1 during Leo season and is the first of the three harvest festivals. The name Lughnasadh originates as a festival in honor of the Irish god, Lugh, while Lammas comes from "Loaf Mass Day" and may have more Christian origins.

Lammas will always hold a special place in my heart as it was the first sabbat I ever celebrated. It's one of the most overlooked sabbats, I think, because early August still feels downright summery, not like harvest season just yet. I love the subtlety of this sabbat, though, how it helps us just start to notice the tiny changes in the seasons—how the plants and animals begin to react as the sun's strength lessens and we move slowly toward fall.

As the first harvest festival, Lammas is a time of gratitude and abundance. It's the sign of our last opportunity to celebrate the summer sunshine and the bounty of our gardens and local produce and the early harvest of wheat, grain, corn, and vegetables. Baking wheat bread or corn bread from scratch are excellent ways to celebrate Lammas and to give thanks to the earth for her abundance. I also love to enjoy the late summer fruits of blackberries, apricots, and plums, which are plentiful this time of year (and delicious on top of fresh baked bread!). Refer to page 140 to learn more about the correspondences of Leo for Lammas as well.

- **Calendar Date:** August 1
- **Astrological Date:** When sun reaches midpoint of Leo season (15° Leo)
- **Lunar Date:** Full moon in Aquarius (could occur anytime between July 20–August 20)
- **Astrological Season:** Leo

- **Alternate Names:** Lughnasadh, Loaf Mass Day, first harvest festival
- **Goddesses:** Ceres (Roman goddess of agriculture), Shala (Sumerian goddess of grain)
- **Crystals:** Carnelian, amber
- **Plants:** Blackberry, corn

*Note: The above information is for the Northern Hemisphere. In the Southern Hemisphere, the festival of Imbolc occurs during Leo season in August. Refer to the Aquarius season and Imbolc sections for correspondences.*

## Autumn Equinox

The autumn equinox is sometimes called Mabon, named for the Welsh sun god, though this is a modern construction. The equinox takes place when the sun moves into Libra. It is the second harvest festival and is all about abundance and gratitude, so that means food! Baking bread and cooking with seasonal squash and fruits are common parts of this celebration, as well as sharing what you're thankful for. Connecting and feasting with your loved ones is another common way to celebrate.

Remember that this is one of the two days of the year (the other being the spring equinox in March) when daylight and nighttime hours are balanced. Because the autumn equinox is always the first day of Libra season, which is represented by the symbol of the scales, the energy of balance is strongly highlighted at this sabbat. This is a good time to reflect on the past six months since the spring equinox and where you're at in terms of progressing toward the goals and intentions you set—and rebalancing work, life, magick, and relationships if needed. Refer to page 166 to learn more about the correspondences of Libra for the autumn equinox as well.

- **Calendar Date:** Approximately September 20 (can shift up to 3 days in either direction)
- **Astrological Date:** When the sun reaches 0° Libra
- **Lunar Date:** Not Applicable
- **Astrological Season:** Libra
- **Alternate Names:** Mabon, Witches' Thanksgiving
- **Goddesses:** Ceres (Roman goddess of agriculture), Pachamama (Incan goddess of earth and crops)
- **Crystals:** Tiger's eye, agate
- **Plants:** Squash, sage

*Note: The above information is for the Northern Hemisphere. In the Southern Hemisphere, the spring equinox occurs when the sun reaches 0° Libra around September 20. Refer to the Aries season and spring equinox sections for correspondences.*

## Samhain

The autumn fire festival is Samhain, which is the early Gaelic and Celtic celebration of Halloween that takes place October 31 during Scorpio season and is the final harvest festival. This festival is sometimes considered to be the "blood harvest," as this was the last chance for hunters in the ancient world to bring home fresh meat to be preserved for winter. There is also a strong connection to magick, ancestral traditions, and the underworld at Samhain. This is demonstrated by Día de los Muertos ("The Day of the Dead"), a holiday celebrated by Latin American cultures just a day later on November 1.

For many witches, Samhain is the most important day of the year and the most important sabbat. It's said that on this day, the veil between worlds is at its thinnest, meaning that ancestors, spirits, faeries, and messages can more easily pass from other worlds into our own. The most traditional and ancient celebrations of Samhain are all about connecting with and honoring our ancestors on this night when they can pass into our world. These traditions include holding a dumb supper, where the table is set with an extra seat and dinner is eaten in reverent silence, making offerings to ancestors, and doing divination to receive messages from beyond.

Other common celebrations include carving faces into vegetables and squash to ward off evil spirits and dressing in disguises so that spirits can pass among us undetected. If these customs sound very familiar, that's because Samhain is the ancient root of modern Halloween festivities! Many witches and pagans celebrate a combination of spiritual and secular activities on this day. Refer to page 178 to learn more about the correspondences of Scorpio for Samhain as well.

- **Calendar Date:** October 31
- **Astrological Date:** When sun reaches midpoint of Scorpio season (15° Scorpio)
- **Lunar Date:** Full moon in Taurus (could occur anytime between October 20–November 20)
- **Astrological Season:** Scorpio
- **Alternate Names:** Halloween, All Hallows' Eve
- **Goddesses:** Hekate (Greek goddess of witchcraft), Hel (Norse goddess of death)
- **Crystals:** Smoky quartz, bloodstone
- **Plants:** Pumpkin, pomegranate

Note: *The above information is for the Northern Hemisphere. In the Southern Hemisphere, the festival of Beltane occurs during Scorpio season in October. Refer to the Taurus season and Beltane sections for correspondences.*

## Winter Solstice

The winter solstice is often called Yule, which originates in the Germanic and Norse traditions. The solstice takes place when the sun moves into Capricorn and is the longest night of the year with the least number of daylight hours, when the sun is at its lowest strength. It is a celebration of the return of the sun because our ancestors knew that from this day forward, the days slowly, slowly start to get longer again.

The winter solstice is another sabbat that has been heavily co-opted by Christian and modern secular festivities, so it is likely recognizable to you as modern Christmas. Common celebrations of the winter solstice include decorating an evergreen tree and hanging evergreen boughs in your home, hanging lights and lighting candles, exchanging gifts, and baking and drinking warm, spiced foods. These festivities are rooted in the idea of celebrating the return of the sun and bringing light and warmth to the darkest, coldest part of the year. Refer to page 208 to learn more about the correspondences of Capricorn for the winter solstice as well.

- **Calendar Date:** Approximately December 20 (can shift up to 3 days in either direction)
- **Astrological Date:** When the sun reaches 0° Capricorn
- **Lunar Date:** Not applicable

- **Astrological Season:** Capricorn
- **Alternate Names:** Yule, Jul
- **Goddesses:** Frau Holle (Norse goddess of snowfall), Beira (Celtic goddess of winter)
- **Crystals:** Clear quartz, garnet
- **Plants:** Holly, evergreen

*Note: The above information is for the Northern Hemisphere. In the Southern Hemisphere, the summer solstice occurs when the sun reaches 0° Capricorn around December 20. Refer to the Cancer season and summer solstice sections for correspondences.*

## Imbolc

The winter fire festival is Imbolc, which takes place February 1 during Aquarius season and is the harbinger of spring, the promise that we will emerge from winter. This is when we first start to see narcissus, daffodils, crocus, and snowdrops peeking up through the snow or mud. Imbolc is often celebrated by lighting lots of white candles and practicing deep, nourishing self-care. It's really our last chance to reflect on all that we have learned about life and about ourselves since the fall harvest and abundance celebrations and since the spring equinox and astrological new year almost a full year ago.

Imbolc is often one of the hardest sabbats for new witches to connect with because its energy is so simple and subtle and because it is so deeply rooted in agricultural and farming practices that are pretty foreign to most of us now. The name Imbolc originates from the Irish Gaelic word "oimelc," meaning "ewe's milk," as this was the time of year when ewes would nurse new lambs, so this sabbat is often celebrated with dairy products. Though most of us may not be familiar with the cycles of lambing and raising sheep, it is certainly a good opportunity for a cheese board or milk bath! Refer to page 219 to learn more about the correspondences of Aquarius for Imbolc as well.

- **Calendar Date:** February 1
- **Astrological Date:** When sun reaches midpoint of Aquarius season (15° Aquarius)
- **Lunar Date:** Full moon in Leo (could occur anytime between January 20–February 20)
- **Astrological Season:** Aquarius
- **Alternate Names:** Candlemas
- **Goddesses:** Brighid (Irish goddess of the hearth), Vesta (Roman goddess of the sacred flame)
- **Crystals:** Celestite, moonstone
- **Plants:** Chamomile, willow

Note: *The above information is for the Northern Hemisphere. In the Southern Hemisphere, the festival of Lammas occurs during Aquarius season in February. Refer to the Leo season and Lammas sections for correspondences.*

As you can see, the history and origins of the eight pagan sabbats vary widely around the world. However, I believe that these eight celebrations together form a powerful way to mark the passage of time, even if they are not wholly ancient! The sun's influence on us and on the earth is profound. Flowing with the changes in the seasons through the astrological signs and the pagan sabbat festivals is one of my favorite ways to channel the power of the sun as the days lengthen and shorten throughout the year.

# Chapter 4

# SPRING

Springtime begins with the astrological new year and aligns with the Maiden aspect of the Triple Goddess (the Maiden, Mother, and Crone). This beautiful time of year is known for blossoming flowers, baby animals, and blustery winds. Energetically, spring is aligned with the element of air. It's a fresh breeze, blowing new opportunities and fresh starts into our lives.

In terms of the seasonal, lunar, and astrological cycles, springtime in the Northern Hemisphere is home to:

- Aries season, which begins at the spring equinox and includes the Aries new moon and Libra full moon.
- Taurus season, which includes the festival of Beltane, the Taurus new moon, and Scorpio full moon.
- Gemini season, which leads us through the transition to summer and includes the Gemini new moon and Sagittarius full moon.

On the following pages, I'm going to share correspondences and recipes to help you embody and be in flow with all of these festivals, lunations, and seasonal rhythms!

*Note: In the Southern Hemisphere, Aries, Taurus, and Gemini seasons occur during autumn. If you live south of the equator, refer to the sections for the opposite signs, Libra, Scorpio, and Sagittarius, for inspiration on celebrating these seasons.*

# ARIES SEASON (LATE MARCH TO APRIL)

Aries season is from approximately March 20 to April 19 each year, though it can shift a few days in either direction. As the first sign in the zodiac, Aries is all about new beginnings and going after what you want. During Aries season, you're likely to feel inspired to set new intentions and goals. Aries season is the start of the astrological new year since this is when the sun is in the first sign of the zodiac. In fact, this is really the best time to be making "new year's resolutions" as opposed to January, which is a much more arbitrary date for the new year!

- **Dates:** March 20–April 19
- **Season:** Spring
- **Element:** Fire
- **Modality:** Cardinal
- **Symbol:** The Ram
- **Archetype:** The Warrior
- **Ruling Planet:** Mars (named for the Roman god of war)
- **Body Part:** Head, face
- **Tarot Card:** The Emperor, The Fool
- **Color:** Red
- **Plants:** Chili pepper, mustard, black pepper, cayenne, cactus
- **Crystals:** Diamond, carnelian

- **Goddesses:** Athena (Greek goddess of war and wisdom), Freya (Norse goddess of war, love, and witchcraft)

Note: *The above information is for the Northern Hemisphere. In the Southern Hemisphere, Aries season, the new moon in Aries, and the full moon in Libra still occur in March and April but herald the beginning of the autumn season instead of spring. Refer to the Libra season section for correspondences, recipes, and rituals.*

## SPRING EQUINOX

The spring equinox is the first day of the first sign in the zodiac. It's a day of balance, when daylight and nighttime hours are equal, and a day of hopefulness. There are fresh, new beginnings in the air at the spring equinox. The spring equinox is traditionally associated with the fertility of the earth, a promise for abundance later in the year, so it's a great time for manifestation work and setting intentions for an abundant year ahead.

When I allow myself to truly dream without limits, what do I wish to manifest into my life this year?

_____

_____

_____

What does it mean to be hopeful about the future?

_____

_____

_____

What is the most abundant, fertile future I can imagine (and how can I take it just one step further)?

_____

_____

_____

## Astrological New Year Intention Setting Tea

Although we typically set intentions at the new moon (and I highly encourage you to set intentions at the fiery new moon in Aries as well), the spring equinox is a great time to set your intentions for the entire year ahead. Think of this as an opportunity to reiterate or redo your new year's resolutions. This intention setting tea is designed to support you in the business of getting clarity on what you're passionate about and zeroing in on some meaningful intentions for the next year.

- 3 parts green tea leaves (for inspiration)
- 2 parts dried lemon verbena (for reinforcing positive habits)
- 2 parts dried lavender (for peace and blessings)
- 1 part dried calendula (for prosperity)
- 1 part dried lemon peel (for cleansing and fresh starts)

Combine all ingredients in a small bowl, then scoop into a tea infuser or empty tea bag. Place the infuser or tea bag in a cup and pour hot water over it. Allow to steep for 1 to 3 minutes. If the weather allows, take your cup of tea outside with a journal. (Alternatively, you could sit by a window.) Find a comfortable spot and take a few deep, cleansing breaths in through your nose and sigh them out through your mouth. Relax your shoulders down your back and become really still and present. Close your eyes and listen to the natural world around you. Become aware of the breeze, chirping birds, or scents of flowers and fresh grass and take a sip of your tea.

When you feel calm and centered, open your eyes and begin to journal on your hopes, dreams, and wishes for the next year, sipping your tea as you write. As you finish the cup of tea, look back over your notes, looking for themes and intentions to emerge. Choose a few things to set as your main intentions for the year; these could be ideals you want to embody, actions you want to take, or goals you want to accomplish. Write them down where you'll be able to see and refer back to them regularly.

## Spring Cleansing Spray

Spring cleaning is a bit of a cliché for a reason: this time of year is perfect for clearing out the old and welcoming the new. Spring cleaning doesn't just mean physical cleaning, either! Although this is a good time to open the windows, wipe away the dust, and air out the house to release the stuffiness of winter, it's also a good time to energetically air out your life. This cleansing spray is a fresh, clean way to bring some energetic life and invigorating scent to your home, office, or altar space.

- 10–15 drops grapefruit essential oil (for purification)
- 10–15 drops lavender essential oil (for purification and prosperity)
- 8–10 drops lemongrass essential oil (for clarity)
- 5–8 drops hyssop essential oil (for purification and clarity)
- 1 ounce alcohol- and fragrance-free witch hazel (for purification)
- ⅓ cup distilled water

Using a dropper, place the essential oils into 1 (4-ounce) amber or cobalt glass jar and top with witch hazel. Add distilled water to fill the container and fit with a spray bottle lid. Shake the bottle to combine, then allow to sit for preferably at least a day or two in a cool place away from sunlight.

Open all the doors and windows in your space. It's okay if you can only open some of them; just try to get as much airflow as possible! Starting on the east side of the room (that's the side of the room that faces the sunrise in the morning), spritz the cleansing spray near the closest door or window and say out loud or silently to yourself: "I cleanse this space of winter's rest and call in a fresh, new beginning." Move around the room counterclockwise. Spritz the cleansing spray into the corners of the room, at each door and window, and anywhere you feel called to, repeating the affirmation above as many times as you desire, until you have returned to the spot in the room where you began, facing east. You might additionally sweep the floors, beginning in the center of the room and sweeping out of the doors to remove and release any lingering, stagnant, or negative energy.

## Plant-Based Colored Egg Dyes

The symbolism of eggs at springtime comes from the Celtic and Germanic celebrations of the spring equinox, which is the precursor to modern-day, secular Easter festivities. Eggs, bunnies, and baby animals are all symbols of fertility, a prominent theme of the spring equinox, when the earth is just beginning to blossom and *spring* forth with new life.

Working with the energy of fertility can feel outdated or uncomfortable if you're not interested in conception or are struggling to conceive, but fertility is an essential part of life that goes far beyond reproduction. You need a fertile imagination in order to pursue your passions and create the life you dream of. Fertility spells can be used to call in inspiration, money, and abundance of all kinds. Coloring eggs with homemade plant-based dyes is a fun way to celebrate the spring equinox and cultivate fertile creativity while honoring and inspiring your inner child as well!

- 3–4 cups water, divided
- ½ head red cabbage for blue eggs (to bring about harmony)
- 3 tablespoons white vinegar, divided
- 1 cup shredded beets for pink eggs (to bring about self-love)
- 1 cup yellow onion skins for orange eggs (to bring about joyfulness)
- 6 hard-boiled eggs with white shells

Place 1½ cups of water in a saucepan and add the cabbage. Bring the water to a boil, then reduce the heat to a simmer for 15 to 30 minutes. Strain the dye into a glass bowl or jar and stir in 1 tablespoon of vinegar. Repeat this process with the remaining two dye colors. Submerge two eggs in each dye color and refrigerate for at least 6 hours and up to 24 hours, until the eggs have reached your desired color. Carefully strain and gently remove the eggs to a tray to dry. Refrigerate until ready to peel and eat.

## NEW MOON IN ARIES

The new moon in Aries is a very potent time for setting intentions because it is the first new moon of the astrological year. It can occur on the spring equinox or up to twenty-eight days later, but the period between the equinox and new moon, however long it may be, is the peak of that astrological new year vibe (new-year-new-moon-new-me). This is a great time to set intentions for the entire year ahead.

What do I want my life to look like for the next year?

_____

_____

_____

Twelve months from now, what do I want to be, have, do, believe, and experience?

_____

_____

_____

How can I embody my inner warrior this month and year, taking empowered, aligned action to achieve my goals?

_____

_____

_____

## Candle Dressing Oil for Inspiration

As you contemplate the year ahead and the goals and intentions you plan to set, you might find yourself needing a spark of inspiration. Working with candles in your magickal practice brings in the element of fire (the element of Aries) and can help you find that spark. This candle dressing oil is designed to inspire you to set bold, aligned intentions for the new moon and the astrological new year.

- 2 teaspoons carrier oil such as sunflower or olive oil
- 2–3 drops grapefruit essential oil (for inspiration)

- 2–3 drops rosemary essential oil (for focus)
- 1–3 drops tea tree essential oil (for enhancing creativity)

Combine the oils in a small bowl, mixing them gently. Alternatively, you could combine them in a bottle fitted with a roller ball cap. Take a white, yellow, or orange birthday or chime candle and hold it in one hand. Dip your fingers in the oil mixture and rub the oil onto the candle, starting from the bottom and working your way up to the middle, then from the top down to the middle. If using a roller ball bottle, simply roll the oil onto the candle from bottom to middle and top to middle. Rubbing the oil into the center of the candle is to call in energy, as opposed to banishing it.

Place the candle in a fire-safe holder and strike a match. As you light the candle, say out loud or silently to yourself: "I invite in the spark of inspiration."

Sit down to contemplate your new moon and astrological new year intentions while the candle burns, perhaps completing the journal prompts above. Try to sit with this for the entire length of time until the candle completely burns out on its own (that's about 20 to 30 minutes for a birthday candle and about an hour or more for a chime candle). However, if you need to get up or leave for any reason, be sure to extinguish the candle and *do not* leave it burning unattended.

Write down your intentions for the month or year ahead on a separate slip of paper and light it on the candle just before it burns out to release your intentions into the universe. However, if you aren't quite ready by the time the candle burns out, you can also burn your intentions with a match or simply write them down in your journal or grimoire. You can also do this little ritual anytime you need inspiration on a project, not just at the new moon in Aries!

# FULL MOON IN LIBRA

The full moon in Libra is a reminder of the need for balance during Aries season. Where Aries is about the self, Libra is about the other and about how we relate to one another. This full moon is perfect for celebrating beauty and relationships, connecting with your most sacred people, and reflecting on the ideal of harmony.

How can I bring more balance into my life this month and year?

_____

_____

_____

Who are my most sacred relationships with? How do they help balance my own energy and gifts?

_____

_____

_____

What do I find most beautiful about myself and others?

_____

_____

_____

## Balanced Self Crystal Elixir

Elixirs are liquid potions used for magick and healing. This crystal elixir features water infused with crystals and herbs ruled by balancing Libra to help you find harmony within yourself. Crystal elixirs are typically meant to be consumed so you can add this to your water or any other beverage! However, you can also use it to water your plants, wash your face, or in a ritual bath.

- Ametrine, amethyst, or citrine crystals (for balance and harmony)
- Glass water bottle or mason jar
- Fresh lilac or freesia flowers (from your own backyard or a friend's is best–do not pick from the side of the road, as these flowers could have fumes and chemicals on them)
- Distilled water

Cleanse the crystals gently with water and a soft cloth, cleaning them of any dust or debris, then place them in the bottom of your glass bottle or jar. Add in one or two stems of the fresh flowers as well. Pour the distilled water over the crystals and flowers so that they are completely submerged. Allow to sit in a window, infusing with both sunlight and moonlight for at least 6 hours but no more than 24 hours. Strain the water through a tea or coffee filter to remove any debris. On the full moon in Libra, use the crystal elixir to make a cup of tea or simply sip the cool water at your altar or while gazing up at the beautiful, brilliant face of the moon.

## TAURUS SEASON [LATE APRIL TO MAY]

Taurus season is from approximately April 20 to May 19 each year, though it can shift a few days in either direction. Taurus is a sensual, pleasure-seeking sign that's all about getting grounded in enjoyment and finding stability. During Taurus season, you may have a tendency to revel more than usual in sensual delights and comforts. You'll just want to lay outside in the sunshine, feel the grass beneath your feet, smell the roses, and enjoy a delicious glass of wine!

- **Dates:** April 20–May 19
- **Season:** Spring
- **Element:** Earth
- **Modality:** Fixed
- **Symbol:** The Bull
- **Archetype:** The Goddess
- **Ruling Planet:** Venus (named for the Roman goddess of love)

- **Body Part:** Neck
- **Tarot Card:** The Empress, Queen of Pentacles
- **Color:** Dark green
- **Goddesses:** Aphrodite (Greek goddess of love), Lakshmi (Hindu goddess of beauty and fertility)
- **Plants:** Rose, oats, strawberry, apple, birch
- **Crystals:** Emerald, jade, rose quartz

Note: *The above information is for the Northern Hemisphere. In the Southern Hemisphere, Taurus season, the new moon in Taurus, and the full moon in Scorpio still occur in April and May but sustain us through the autumn season instead of spring. Refer to the Scorpio season section for correspondences, recipes, and rituals.*

# BELTANE

Beltane is the fire festival of the goddess. It's all about fertility, sexuality, and sensual embodiment. Beltane also has a connection to the fae, as it's believed to be one of the two nights of the year when the veil between worlds is at its thinnest (the other day being Samhain during Scorpio season). There is love and magick in the air at Beltane, making it a perfect time for love or self-love magick and sensual delights.

How can I embody self-love more fully and deeply?

_____

_____

_____

What does it mean to celebrate my sensuality and/or sexuality?

_____

_____

_____

How does it feel to receive all of my deepest, most grounded desires?

_____

_____

_____

## Rosewater Facial Toner for Self-Love

This simple toner is one of the first herbal recipes I ever made for myself and is still a favorite to this day. Rose and frankincense are both great for your skin, as they have anti-inflammatory properties that reduce redness and puffiness. They also pack a magickal punch, as rose is an almost universal ally for love and self-love and frankincense has been a favorite spiritual oil for millennia.

Rosewater is a hydrosol (water infused with plant material); in this case, rose petals. It's been used as a skin-care product for centuries (and that's no surprise to me, since it smells amazing and feels even better). A quick spritz of this refreshing, enlivening blend when you step out of the shower or after washing your face will brighten your whole day—magickally and cosmetically.

- 2 ounces distilled water
- 1 ounce alcohol- and fragrance-free witch hazel (for purification)
- 1 ounce rosewater (for self-love)
- 8–10 drops frankincense essential oil (for positive vibrations)

Combine all ingredients in a glass bottle fitted with a spray cap and gently shake to combine. Spritz on damp skin after cleansing or showering for a refreshing dose of hydration and self-love.

Most of us take a shower quite a bit more than we draw a full bubble bath, yet we miss this great opportunity for magick. Although they might not be quite as inherently romantic as a ritual bath, a ritual shower is definitely a thing and just as magickal and potent! Try this little ritual the next time you're needing a self-love boost, especially during Taurus season and around Beltane. Turn the faucet on and allow it to run until warm. Spritz two or three pumps of rosewater toner into the steam to infuse your shower experience with self-love vibes. As you cleanse your body and hair, imagine that you're not only cleaning away dirt or sweat but also negativity, doubt, fear, shame, and self-critical thoughts. Watch those thoughts and energies wash off your body and swirl down the drain, leaving you free of their weight. As you finish your shower, imagine a cleansing pink or golden light pouring down from the faucet above, washing over you and flooding you with positivity until your skin glows.

Shut off the water and step out of the shower, drying off. Take a moment to watch the last of the water—and any negativity or heaviness you've been feeling—drain away. Gently pat your face dry with a towel, then spritz three to four pumps of rosewater toner on your cheeks, chin, and forehead. Feel the cool, soothing, yet brightening sensation of the rose, witch hazel, and frankincense on your skin, sealing in self-love for the rest of the day.

## Handmade Flower Crown

As Beltane is the opposite point in the year from Samhain, when the veil between worlds is at its thinnest, it's believed that faeries and spirit

guides are more active and prevalent this time of year. Flower crowns are synonymous with the springtime sabbats, especially Beltane. There's nothing that makes you feel more magickal, whimsical, and fae-like than adorning yourself with fresh flowers!

Making flower crowns is surprisingly easy and a lot of fun. These make a great Beltane craft project with kids, for a girls' night, as well as weddings and other festivities. You can use just about any flower in your crown, but I recommend daisies, anemones, wax flower, spray roses, and other small or flat blossoms that will last so you can enjoy your flower crown for a few days.

- Soft sewing tape measure
- Wire cutters
- Floral wire
- Floral tape
- Fresh or silk flowers, cut to individual stems about 4–6 inches long
- Colorful ribbons (optional)

With a soft sewing tape measure, measure the circumference of your head approximately where you'd like to wear the flower crown (i.e., sitting straight on top, tilted up, etc.). With wire cutters, cut your floral wire to a length of about three or four inches longer than the total circumference needed, then bend it into a circle. Pull it to the circumference you measured, then wrap the remaining wire around itself to close the circle. Wrap the closed section securely with floral tape to protect any sharp edges.

Place stems of flowers along the wire, wrapping each stem securely with flower tape. Place each flower snug next to the one beside it to create a lush, full appearance. When you've wrapped stems all the way around the crown, spritz it lightly with a spray bottle of cool water and store it in a cool place such as on a tile bathroom floor (but not as cold as in a refrigerator). Add colored ribbons to the back for even more faery-inspired fun!

## Rose Quartz-Infused Sparkling Strawberry Lemonade

This sweet, tart, effervescent concoction combines several of my favorite flavors. Strawberries and lemons are a classic combination because they are simply delicious and their sweet, tart flavors balance each other perfectly. They both also happen to support luck in love and friendship, so these two have all the feel-good vibes.

Beltane is the first fire festival of the astrological year. Fire festivals were traditionally celebrated by the ancient Celts with bonfires and community gatherings. Beltane, in particular, was a time of weddings and handfastings (engagements), so there was often much to celebrate. Sparkling beverages have been a mainstay of celebratory events for hundreds, if not thousands, of years, from the mead of ancient India and Greece to French Champagne originating in the eighteenth and nineteenth centuries. You can make this Beltane potion with the sparkling beverage of your choice to celebrate life and love!

- 4 cups water, divided
- 1 cup sugar
- 2 cups fresh-squeezed lemon juice (for love and friendship)
- 8–12 fresh strawberries (for luck in love)
- 5 small rose quartz crystals

- collins glasses for serving
- Champagne or sparkling water (for celebration)

In a small saucepan, combine 2 cups of water and the sugar. Bring to a boil, then reduce to a simmer until the sugar is dissolved and the liquid is clear. Remove from heat and allow to cool. Strain the fresh lemon juice into a pitcher. Top with the cooled simple syrup and the remaining water or to taste. Add ice and chill.

Rinse and pat the strawberries and rose quartz crystals dry. Place the rose quartz crystals on your cutting board or kitchen counter, with one crystal in each cardinal direction (North, South, East, and West) and one crystal centered above the others, so they form the points of a five-point star or pentagram. As you slice the strawberries, focus on imbuing them with love and celebration. Place the slices inside the rose quartz pentagram grid. When all the strawberries are sliced, hold your hands over the grid and imagine light rising up out of the crystals to infuse the fruit with their loving energy. Additionally, or alternatively, you could make a rose quartz crystal elixir to use as the water in your lemonade! When ready to serve, place 5 to 8 strawberry slices in the bottom of each glass. Pour your lemonade over the strawberries, then top with Champagne or sparkling water.

## NEW MOON IN TAURUS

The new moon in Taurus is a time for pleasure and total embodiment of your goals. Where Aries is action and creation, Taurus is here to help you receive the rewards of your hard work. Consider setting intentions at this new moon around how to receive more of what you truly desire and create space for more ease and pleasure in your life.

Where in my life do I want to experience more pleasure and more ease?

_____

_____

_____

How does my inner goddess want me to start embodying my goals and desires as if they are already here?

_____

_____

_____

What would it look like for life to feel easy and pleasant?

_____

_____

_____

# Inner Goddess Rosebud Tea

Rosebud tea is one of my personal favorites, perhaps because I'm a Taurus sun myself! It's one of few plants that seems to have an almost universal meaning and magickal correspondence. Just about everyone agrees that roses = love. Roses have been associated with love goddesses back into the depths of history and mythology, including Venus, Aphrodite, Isis, and even Mary Magdalene. Every zodiac sign is associated with a myriad of archetypes, human characters that symbolize the energy of that sign. Taurus is ruled by Venus and associated with other love and fertility goddesses since they embody pleasure and receiving what you desire.

There are two edible portions of the rose: the petals or buds and the fruit, known as rose hips, which are small, almost berry-like formations that grow at the base of a rose blossom. Rose petals and rosebuds are sweetly floral, while rose hips have more of a tart flavor. This tea combines both rosebuds and rose hips for extra loving, heart-opening energy!

- 2 parts green tea leaves (for inspiration)
- 2 parts dried rosebuds (for love)
- 1 part dried rose hips (for opening the heart)
- 1 part dried elderflower (for channeling divine feminine wisdom)
- 1 part marshmallow root (for encouraging gentleness)
- dried hibiscus petals, to taste (for love and lust)

Combine all ingredients in a small bowl and gently mix to combine. Scoop into tea bag(s), depending on number of servings, or store loose tea in a glass jar. When ready to enjoy, place a tea bag or tea infuser filled with loose tea in your cup. Boil water and pour over tea bag or tea infuser. Allow to steep 3 to 5 minutes.

At the new moon in Taurus, brew a cup of this tea and put on an outfit that makes you feel gorgeous and sensual. Create a cozy little nest of blankets and pillows on your bed or sofa, light lots of candles, and enjoy a deliciously indulgent cookie or treat with your tea as you contemplate your new moon intentions and complete the journal prompts above.

## FULL MOON IN SCORPIO

The full moon in Scorpio is a reminder that although not everything in life is quite as easy as Taurus might prefer, we do have the power to transform even pain and shadows into beauty. Where Taurus is about pleasure, Scorpio is about potency and finding magick in the darkest parts of life. This full moon is perfect for practicing magick and witchcraft, working with your divination tools, and doing some shadow work.

How can I embrace my personal power more potently?

_____

_____

_____

What shadows (blocks, fears, or limiting beliefs) are currently rising to the surface for me to examine?

_____

_____

_____

What steps can I take to transmute my shadows into beautiful strengths?

_____

_____

_____

## Love Spell Anointing Oil

Love spells are a point of contention in the modern witchcraft community. Many witches believe that love spells inherently impact someone's free will and should never be practiced, while others believe that all magick has a rightful place in their repertoire. I personally choose not to cast love spells on other people, but I do believe that there's nothing wrong with casting a love spell on yourself! This could be a spell to help you love yourself more deeply and unconditionally or to open your heart to receiving love from others. The full moon in Scorpio is a great time to cast love spells like this for a number of reasons. First of all, Taurus is the season of love and sensuality, ruled by the goddess of love herself, and Scorpio is the sign of magick, witchcraft, and spell work. Scorpio is also the sign of shadows and navigating your personal underworld of fear, doubt, grief, and pain. What could be more supportive of that process of transformation than also opening your heart to love and self-love? Plus, the full moon is a time of abundance and amplification, making it the perfect time to amplify your love for yourself and others.

- 2 teaspoons pomegranate seed oil or other carrier oil (for loving your shadows)
- 3 drops rose essential oil* (for opening your heart)

_____

* You can substitute rose geranium essential oil for rose oil if you prefer, as rose oil can be quite expensive.

- 3 drops cardamom essential oil (for intimacy)
- rose quartz chips (optional)

Combine all ingredients in a small bowl or glass bottle fitted with a roller ball cap. Gently stir or shake to combine. Hold your hands on either side of the bowl or bottle and clear your mind. Envision a soft golden or pink light filling the space between your hands, swirling with energy and the pure, potent vibration of love. Imagine it infusing the oil with this vibration, staying here until you feel that the oil is complete. You might also charge the oil under the light of the full moon in Scorpio for a night before performing your spell.

To amplify your ritual, light some pink or white candles and create a love or self-love altar. You could make a rose quartz crystal grid on your altar, wear rose quartz jewelry, or hold a rose quartz in one hand while you anoint yourself. You might also want to bring in the shadowy Scorpio energy by creating a protective barrier around yourself and your altar with an energetic shield or smoky quartz crystals. Dress in soft, flowing clothing that makes you feel sensual and sexy. Find a comfortable seat and relax, taking a deep breath in through your nose and sighing it out through your mouth. Place one hand over your heart and the other over your belly, womb, or your third eye. Take a few deep, cleansing breaths, closing your eyes and tuning into your body. Breathe into tension wherever you feel it and allow it to release, letting it know that it is safe to do so.

When you feel ready, dip your fingertips in the oil and anoint your third eye, saying out loud or silently to yourself, "I see love all around." Dip your fingertips in the oil again and anoint the inside of your wrists, saying out loud or silently to yourself, "I give and receive love freely." Dip your fingertips in the oil one more time and anoint your sternum, above your heart, saying out loud or silently to yourself, "I am open to love. I *am* love." This would be a perfect time to move into a meditation or spirit guide journey to receive guidance from your higher self or to visualize what it feels like to love yourself unconditionally or to receive love abundantly.

# GEMINI SEASON [LATE MAY TO JUNE]

Gemini season is from approximately May 20 to June 19 each year, though it can shift a few days in either direction. Gemini is a playful, curious, creative sign that's all about communication and knowledge. During Gemini season, it's common to feel looser and more flexible than at other times of the year, and we tend to be extra sociable! This is a great time for parties, prioritizing time with friends, and sharing ideas that you're passionate about. The deeper lesson of Gemini, though, is that you have the power to adapt to your reality and to adapt your reality to suit your needs.

- **Dates:** May 20–June 19
- **Season:** Spring
- **Element:** Air
- **Modality:** Mutable
- **Symbol:** The Twins
- **Archetype:** The Magician
- **Ruling Planet:** Mercury (named for the Roman messenger god)
- **Body Part:** Shoulders, arms, hands, lungs
- **Tarot Cards:** The Magician, The Lovers
- **Color:** Yellow
- **Goddesses:** Circe (Greek demi-goddess of sorcery), Itzpapalotl (Aztec Obsidian Butterfly goddess)

- **Plants:** Lavender, mint, bergamot, lemon verbena
- **Crystals:** Blue lace agate, chrysocolla

*Note: The above information is for the Northern Hemisphere. In the Southern Hemisphere, Gemini season, the new moon in Gemini, and the full moon in Sagittarius still occur in May and June but lead us through the transition from autumn to winter, instead of from spring to summer. Refer to the Sagittarius season section for correspondences, recipes, and rituals.*

# TRANSITION FROM SPRING TO SUMMER

The mutable signs are like liminal spaces, transitions from one season to the next, existing in both and neither. Gemini season is the transition from spring to summer, from hope to action. It's one last chance to finalize your plans and set things in motion before we head into the fiery motivation of summertime. There is a bubbly, social energy about Gemini season, so you might feel called to connect with friends and share more of your thoughts. This is the perfect time to check in with yourself and to communicate what you need in order to feel nurtured and safe.

How can I more effectively communicate what I need in my relationships?

_____

_____

_____

What plans do I need to finalize before summer arrives?

_____

_____

_____

Are there any updates I want to make to my plans, ideas, or thoughts?

_____

_____

_____

## Lavender Sugar for Social Connections

When I was in high school, my mom briefly owned a cupcake shop in our small town. It was long hours and late nights of baking, but I loved coming up with creative recipes for the cupcakes, scones, and other pastries we sold. Seasonal and holiday recipes were my favorite; given the topic of this book, I guess some things never really change. Because we also owned a flower shop (we were busy!), we loved incorporating edible flowers into our spring and summertime recipes.

Though it's been many years since I worked behind the pink-and-white striped counter of our "cupcakerie," I still have a few recipes

from those days that I still make quite often. One of my favorites is this lavender sugar recipe that we used to use in scones, tarts, and frosting! It's unbelievably simple to make and lends a sweet, deliciously playful floral note to your baked goods or even your morning tea or coffee. As we transition from spring to summer, use this lavender sugar to connect with the playful, sociable energy of Gemini over a cup of tea with a friend.

- 1½ cups white sugar
- ½ cup dried lavender flowers (for peace and calm)

Using a small blender or an immersion blender, combine the sugar and lavender, mixing well. (Blending the sugar and flowers will mingle their flavors more completely than stirring and will grind the sugar into finer, more powdery crystals.) Place the combined sugar and flowers in a glass jar and store in a cool, dry place. When ready to use, simply stir the sugar into your baked goods or tea or coffee. When baking, I recommend only substituting a few tablespoons of sugar with this flavored sugar, otherwise the lavender flavor can be overpowering.

The next time you have a friend over for tea, serve this delicious treat! Gemini loves to socialize and to be in conversation with others, so sitting down with a friend over tea, cookies, and lavender sugar is sure to sweeten your conversation and aid in inspiring wit, humor, and meaningful connection. For an extra dose of magick to inspire words of wisdom and hilarity, charge the jar of lavender sugar under the dark night of the new moon in Gemini.

## Communication Clarity Diffuser Blend (and Breathwork)

Gemini is symbolized by the Twins, which not only represent both the duality and changeability of this sign, but also the fact that Gemini loves to be in conversation with others. During Gemini season, we all get a little dose of this chatty, social vibe and tend to want to share our thoughts and ideas more than usual. However, sometimes we all need a little help communicating effectively. Luckily, Gemini energy is here to support and empower you with clarity in your communications!

Whether you're struggling to be understood or there's a little trickster energy in the air during Mercury retrograde (which happens three times a year), this essential oil diffuser blend will infuse your home or office space with clarity. This is an ideal blend to diffuse before a challenging conversation or during a meeting where complex subjects will be discussed.

- 4 drops hyssop essential oil (for mental clarity)
- 3 drops lemongrass essential oil (for intuitive clarity)
- 2 drops peppermint essential oil (for communication)

Combine all ingredients in water in an ultrasonic diffuser or in a reed diffuser and allow the bright, vibrant scents to infuse your space. If you have time, do some breathwork for the first five to ten minutes that the oils are diffusing. If you're feeling anxious about a difficult conversation or about being misunderstood, try this breathing technique to help calm the nervous system:

1. Close your eyes, relax your shoulders, and let all your breath out.
2. Breathe in through your nose for the count of 4.
3. Hold it at the top for the count of 4.
4. Breathe slowly out through your mouth for the count of 8.
5. Repeat at least 2 to 3 more times or as many times as you need until you feel grounded and calm.

If you're feeling scattered and having trouble focusing on the conversation at hand, try this breathing technique to bring your attention back to your breath and your body:

1. Close your eyes, relax your shoulders, and let all your breath out.
2. Take a deep breath in through your nose, filling your lungs and your belly all the way up.
3. Sigh it out through your mouth, releasing tension and stress as you do.
4. Take another deep breath in through your nose.
5. Sigh it out through your mouth, this time opening your mouth and actively breathing it out.
6. Take one more deep breath in through your nose.
7. Sigh it out through your mouth, exhaling and sighing out loud, vocalizing any stress or tension that remains and expelling it from your body.

## Lavender Mint Whipped Body & Hand Butter

Gemini rules the shoulders, arms, hands, and lungs—the parts of our bodies that help us to breathe and communicate our thoughts and feelings. During Gemini season, it's an especially good idea to nourish these body parts as they are called into focus by the cosmic cycles. This lavender mint body butter is made with ingredients ruled by Gemini to nourish your skin both energetically and physically.

I used to pretty much only stick with teas and oil blends in my at-home herbalism practice, but when I discovered how easy it actually is to make my own creams and body butters, a whole new world opened up for me! Especially if you have an immersion blender, these creams are incredibly simple and satisfying to make and to gift. This particular recipe is especially lovely applied after the shower or just before bed so that it has time to really soak into your skin and nourish it overnight.

- ½ cup shea butter
- ¼ cup coconut oil
- ¼ cup olive oil
- 1 teaspoon vitamin E oil
- 15 drops lavender essential oil (for peace and calm)
- 5 drops peppermint essential oil (for clear thinking)
- immersion or hand blender

In a double boiler, melt shea butter and coconut oil, stirring gently with a spatula. Remove from heat and allow to cool slightly, then gently stir in olive oil, vitamin E oil, and essential oils. Place the bowl in the freezer for 1 to 2 hours until it solidifies but is not rock-hard. Remove from the freezer and place the immersion or hand blender into the solidified cream. Whip until the entire bowl is light and fluffy. Store in a glass jar in a cool place.

When you want to use the body butter, scoop a small amount into your palm and rub into your skin gently but firmly, focusing on the motion.

Rub it into your palms, then give special attention to each finger in turn, maybe working up over your wrists and arms as well. When you are finished, cup your hands over your face and inhale deeply of the clean, calming scent of lavender and peppermint to nourish your mind as well as your body.

## NEW MOON IN GEMINI

The new moon in Gemini is a time for socializing and gathering information. Gemini is all about communication, so this is a great time to open up some honest conversations, share your feelings and perspective, and start journaling in earnest. Consider setting intentions at this new moon around allowing more space for flexibility in your life.

Where in my life do I want to be more flexible and adaptable?

_____

_____

_____

How can I be more adaptable to my reality but also adapt my reality to suit my own needs and goals?

_____

_____

_____

What social groups do I want to connect with more in the next month?

_____

_____

_____

## The Magician Tea + Tarot Spread

Every zodiac sign is associated with many different archetypes. I like to associate Gemini with the archetype of the Magician, which is one that I think often

| Card Above | **The Magician** | Card Below |

gets misunderstood. The Magician—and Gemini, by extension—is all about adaptability. Unlike witches, who are associated with transformation, magicians do not necessarily change everything about themselves or their surroundings from the inside out. Rather, they adapt and shift, they allow subtle changes to ripple through their lives and their very being until everything around them has adapted to suit their needs.

There is a playful, mercurial quality to the Magician and an air of curiosity. This is the embodiment of magickal Gemini energy, which can adapt to any situation and can adapt any reality to their liking. This tea blend is designed to inspire that playful curiosity and the belief that you truly can grow and become anything you can dream up—rather like Alice growing very small or very tall while visiting Wonderland.

- 3 parts Earl Grey tea (for power and increasing success)
- 2 parts dried peppermint (for inspiring change)
- 1 part dried lemon verbena (for purification)
- 1 part dried mugwort (for astral travel and visualization)

Combine all ingredients in a small bowl and gently mix to combine. Scoop into tea bag(s), depending on number of servings, or store loose tea in a glass jar. When ready to enjoy, place a tea bag or tea infuser filled with loose tea in your cup. Boil water and pour over tea bag or tea infuser. Allow to steep 3 to 5 minutes.

At the new moon in Gemini, brew a cup of this tea and collect your tarot cards. Shuffle the deck until you feel intuitively called to stop, then flip through the cards until you find The Magician. Place it on the table or altar in front of you, facing up. Place the card that was above The Magician in the deck to the left and the card that was below The Magician in the deck to the right, both facing down for now.

Sip your tea, savoring the bright citrus and mint flavors as you contemplate The Magician. What do this card and this archetype mean to you? What images, thoughts, feelings, sounds, or scents are conjured up by them? What imagery stands out to you in the card and why? When you feel ready, turn over the card to the left. This card represents the power and ability you have to change your reality when you clearly focus and direct your energy. Then, turn over the card to the right. This card represents what you may need to shift internally in order to adapt your own behaviors, talents, strengths, and choices to the boundaries of your reality. As you continue to sip your tea, journal or even record yourself thinking out loud about this reading and what revelations come through for you.

Alternatively, if you do not work with tarot cards, you can simply meditate on the magician archetype and the concepts of change, adaptability, and creating the right circumstances for your desires to manifest.

## FULL MOON IN SAGITTARIUS

The full moon in Sagittarius is a reminder that you have all the wisdom you truly need inside of yourself. While Gemini embodies a love of research and wonderment, Sagittarius embodies a deep, inner knowing of the truth. This full moon is perfect for getting out in the wilderness to connect with yourself and to find answers from within.

How can I trust my inner wisdom more fully?

_____

_____

_____

What answers have I been seeking from outside of myself that I need to turn within to find?

_____

_____

_____

Where do I feel most at peace and able to hear my own thoughts?

_____

_____

_____

## Smoke Cleansing Bundle for Intuitive Wisdom

From saining in Celtic countries to indigenous North American smudging practices, smoke cleansing is a tradition found in regions and spiritual practices all over the world. This is the practice of cleansing our spaces and auras with sacred smoke, clearing away and banishing negativity, and inviting in positive frequencies, spirits, and ideas.

It has become very common to see bundles of white sage sold as "smudge sticks" in New Age shops and even mainstream department stores. Although smoke cleansing is a near-universal concept, the term "smudging" specifically describes an indigenous cleansing ritual, so if you are not indigenous yourself and did not learn directly from an indigenous teacher or healer, it is cultural appropriation to use this term to describe your practices. Instead, you can use the term smoke cleansing or another term drawn from your own ancestry, such as saining if you are of Celtic descent. Luckily, there are many other cleansing herbs that are acceptable and accessible to use! These include common garden sage (which is just as effective as white sage), rosemary, cedar, pine, fir, lavender, and mint, just to name a few.

This smoke cleansing bundle is designed to help you clear your space and aura and invite in your own intuitive wisdom. Sagittarius, as the opposite sign of Gemini, is the sign of the healer. While Gemini is the holder of knowledge and playfully adapts to any situation, Sagittarius is the holder of wisdom and actively creates new situations in which to share and receive. This smoke bundle represents the duality of these two beautiful energies, even down to the elements. Fiery Sagittarius lights the bundle with flame, while airy Gemini carries the sacred smoke on the breeze.

- 3–5 stems fresh, common garden sage (for purification and wisdom)
- 3–5 stems fresh rosemary (for purification and clarity)
- 3–5 stems fresh lavender (for purification and peace)
- 2–3 stems fresh jasmine flowers (for intuition)
- 1–3 small cedar branches (for purification and protection)
- plain twine

Lay all the herbs on a table together and trim to the same length, about six inches. Lay three pieces of twine on the table, about an inch and a half apart, and lay the herbs across them. Tie the twine around the herbs securely, knot, and trim off the ends. Hang your bundle to dry for a week or two.

On the full moon in Sagittarius, find a comfortable spot at your altar or somewhere else in your home or outside. Place a fire-safe bowl or shell on the table in front of you. You might also want to set up some candles, crystals, or other items connected to Sagittarius. Using a match or lighter, light the end of the smoke cleansing bundle so that smoke begins to emerge from it. If it physically lights with flame, gently blow it out.

Hold the bundle in front of you and speak out loud or to yourself, "I cleanse this space of heaviness, of negativity, and of close-mindedness." Wave the smoke gently around you, perhaps walking into different corners of the room in a counterclockwise motion, repeating the affirmation. Return to your seat and hold the bundle in front of you again. Speak out loud or to yourself, "I cleanse myself of doubt and of any disbelief in my own wisdom." Wave the smoke gently around your body, breathing in deeply. When you feel ready, begin to call in intuitive wisdom to fill the newly cleansed space. Wave the smoke into the corners of the room, moving around the room in a clockwise motion this time, speaking out loud or to yourself, "I call in intuitive wisdom from my higher self, from my ancestors, and from the divine. I open myself to receive guidance from within."

Place the bundle in the fire-safe bowl and take this opportunity to meditate, journal, or pull tarot cards or use another divination tool. Relight the bundle as necessary and when you are finished, extinguish it safely. Do not leave the bundle burning if you need to leave the room.

## Chapter 5

# SUMMER

Summertime is the peak of active, fiery energy in the seasonal cycle and aligns with the Mother aspect of the Triple Goddess. This time of year is known for abundant sunshine, deliciously juicy fruits ripe for picking, and lazy days of rest and relaxation. Energetically, summer is aligned with the element of fire. It's a sparkler of fun and play that helps you reconnect with your inner child.

In terms of the seasonal, lunar, and astrological cycles, summertime in the Northern Hemisphere is home to:

- Cancer season, which begins at the summer solstice, and includes the Cancer new moon and Capricorn full moon.
- Leo season, which includes the festival of Lammas, the Leo new moon, and Aquarius full moon.
- Virgo season, which leads us through the transition to autumn, and includes the Virgo new moon and Pisces full moon.

On the following pages, I'm going to share correspondences and recipes to help you embody and be in flow with all of these festivals, lunations, and seasonal rhythms!

Note: *In the Southern Hemisphere, Cancer, Leo, and Virgo seasons occur during autumn. If you live south of the equator, refer to the sections of the opposite signs, Capricorn, Aquarius, and Pisces, for inspiration on celebrating these.*

# CANCER SEASON (LATE JUNE TO JULY)

Cancer season is from approximately June 20 to July 19 each year, though it can shift a few days in either direction. Cancer is a nurturing, emotional, and sensitive sign that's all about self-care and rest.

During Cancer season, you tend to have more direct access to your emotions and intuition than usual because Cancer is the only sign ruled by the moon. It might be a time of heightened emotions or time for a good cry. But Cancer season is also the brightest and sunniest part of the year when the sun is at its peak. This paradox of the sun and moon in conversation is a beautiful one to meditate on.

- **Dates:** June 20–July 19
- **Season:** Summer
- **Element:** Water
- **Modality:** Cardinal
- **Symbol:** The Crab
- **Archetype:** The Mother
- **Ruling Planet:** Moon
- **Body Part:** Chest, breasts, stomach, womb, ovaries
- **Tarot Card:** The High Priestess, The Moon
- **Color:** Silver
- **Goddesses:** Ceres (Roman goddess of agriculture and abundance), Changxi (Chinese goddess of the moon)

- **Plants:** Jasmine, lemon, eucalyptus, aloe, succulents, willow
- **Crystals:** Moonstone, selenite

Note: *The above information is for the Northern Hemisphere. In the Southern Hemisphere, Cancer season, the new moon in Cancer, and the full moon in Capricorn still occur in June and July but herald the beginning of the winter season instead of summer. Refer to the Capricorn season section for correspondences, recipes, and rituals.*

# SUMMER SOLSTICE

The summer solstice is the longest day of the year, when the sun is at the peak of its power. There is almost a pause at the solstices, when time and the earth seem to stand still for a few days, while the difference in daylight hours seems almost imperceptible. These are quite magickal times for that reason! Watching the sunrise and sunset on the solstice is a magickal experience, whether you're doing so at Stonehenge, Machu Picchu, or in your own backyard. It's a celebration of the light of the sun and of the light within your heart.

What lights me up and makes me feel alive?

_____

_____

_____

How can I create more joyful experiences in my everyday life?

_____

_____

_____

When do I feel at the peak or zenith of my own power and strength?

_____

_____

_____

## Moonwater Sun Tea

Moonwater is one of the first spells or recipes that many new witches learn because it's incredibly easy and keeps a low profile (if you're not ready to jump out of the broom closet just yet). So, what is moonwater? Essentially, it's water that's been "charged" by the energy of moonlight. When an object or ingredient is charged with a particular energy, it's infused with the power of that energy; you can think of it like charging up a solar battery. You can charge just about anything: water, other liquids, oil blends, herbal blends, crystals, tarot decks, divination tools, etc. Charging items under the full moon is particularly popular, given that it is the most intuitive and magickal of the four moon phases, but you can actually charge items under any moon phase or astrological transit to align with its energy.

Cancer season is the season of the luminaries in many ways. It begins with the summer solstice, the day of the year when the sun is at its peak, and it is the only astrological sign ruled by the moon. Both the sun and moon are in the fullest expression of their potency during this time of year. You can make moonwater anytime, but this particular blend is charged up with the power of both the moon and the sun to harness and channel the brilliant energy of both cosmic luminaries.

- 4 cups distilled water
- 3 tablespoons white peony tea leaves (for intuition)

- 3 teaspoons dried jasmine flowers (for intuitive connection)
- 3–5 slices dried nectarine* (for hopefulness)
- 1 lemon, sliced (for purification)

Fill a pitcher or large mason jar with the distilled water and top with a tight-fitting lid. Place the jar outside in a safe, protected location or inside on a windowsill. Allow the water to charge in the moonlight all night (regardless of whether you can actually see the moon). Some witches prefer to bring the charged water in before the sunlight touches it, but that's entirely up to you (and in this case, we'll be charging it in the sun, too, so it really doesn't matter).

Combine the tea ingredients in a small bowl and scoop into three empty tea bags. Place the tea bags in the moonwater and place the lid on once more. Place the jar or pitcher outside in a warm, sunny spot, preferably on the summer solstice itself. This will both charge the water with the power of the sun at its peak, but will also slowly warm the water, gently infusing it with the flavor of the tea. When the tea has reached your desired strength (it will likely be quite light in color), bring the jar or pitcher inside and chill in the refrigerator. Serve over ice with lemon slices. This tea is perfect for sipping on a hot summer day or a warm, moonlit night!

---

\* You can purchase dried or dehydrated nectarines at most specialty grocery stores but you can also make them yourself! Simply slice a nectarine into quarters and remove the pit. Place the fruit on a baking sheet, cut sides up, and bake at 225°F for 1½ to 4 hours (depending on size of fruit) until dry and shriveled. Dice into smaller pieces before adding to tea bags.

Aside from making tea, you can also use moonwater for lots of other fun and magickal purposes such as:

- Ritual baths
- Making coffee
- Watering plants
- Rinsing hands, clothes, or dishes for extra purification
- Floating candles on your altar
- And pretty much anything else you use water for!

## Watermelon Sorbet for Emotional Cleansing

Cancer rules plants that are very high in water content, like aloe and succulents, because it's believed that the moon's gravitational pull impacts the water in these plants just as it impacts the ocean's tides. Watermelon is one such plant! Being that it is filled with water and is sweet and refreshing, watermelon is associated with cleansing and purification. This watermelon sorbet is the perfect emotional palate cleanser to usher in the summer solstice as a fresh start and a fresh new season.

- fresh watermelon, cut into chunks (for emotional cleansing)
- optional: 1 cup granulated sugar and 1 cup water
- fresh mint leaves (for purification)

Cut the watermelon into chunks and puree in a food processor or with an immersion blender. If you prefer a sweeter sorbet, make a simple syrup by dissolving the sugar in the water in a small saucepan over medium heat. When the liquid is completely clear, remove from heat and allow to cool. Add the simple syrup to the pureed watermelon and blend until just combined. Scoop into a container with a lid and freeze for at least 6 to 8 hours. Occasionally, you might want to fluff the sorbet with a fork so that it does not freeze too hard or solid (making it difficult to scoop). When you are ready to serve, scoop the sorbet into glass bowls and garnish with a fresh mint leaf.

Before you sit down to enjoy your delicious watermelon treat, especially on or near the solstice, take a moment to write down anything you want to release and cleanse from the previous season or beyond. This might include heavy emotions, traumas, painful conversations, or betrayals. Journal out what you want to release and why it's time to let these thoughts or experiences go.

Enjoy your watermelon sorbet in the sunshine, taking time to savor the fresh flavor, and allow the watermelon to work its magick, cleansing your aura and energy of whatever you choose to release. Afterward, journal on the new, revitalized emotions and experiences you are ready to have in their place.

## Pressed Flowers

Summertime flowers are abundant and beautiful; don't you wish they would last just a little bit longer? I've always loved pressing flowers, ever since I was a little girl. As I mentioned, my mom owned a flower shop when I was growing up, so we always had an abundance of flowers on hand. I remember having some kind of wooden flower press at one time, but simply pressing them between the pages of my mom's coffee table books was my favorite. I would try so hard not to peek or disturb them for at least a week, much as I wanted to! When they were finished, I would turn them into bookmarks and tuck them in special nooks and crannies to be unexpectedly found in the future and inspire delight.

- flowers of your choice
- scissors
- wax paper
- heavy book(s)

Choose your flowers intuitively or based on those that align with a particular magickal intention. With your scissors, snip off the stems at the very base of each flower so that the blossom is as flat as possible. Cut a piece of wax paper and open a heavy book to a center page. Fold the wax paper in half and lay it open inside the book. Place your flowers on the right side of the wax paper so that they are face up. Carefully close the book over the flowers, being sure that they stay flat between the piece of wax paper. Press down firmly on the book, then place it in a safe location where it can remain undisturbed for a week or up to 2 to 3 weeks. You might want to stack additional heavy books on top of it, especially if the flowers are fairly thick or bulky.

After a week, check on the flowers to see if they are sufficiently dried and flattened. If not, allow to press for another 1 to 2 weeks. Once the flowers are dried, remove them from the book and use for decoration or in another craft project. You can place dried flowers under glass and display them, string them into a decorative garland or flower chain, or even glue them into your grimoire.

# NEW MOON IN CANCER

The new moon in Cancer is the first new moon of summer, as it always takes place on or within a few weeks of the summer solstice. This is a time for celebrating your own emotional sensitivity and intuition.

Consider setting intentions this new moon around feeling safe to share your emotions and connect with your intuition.

How can I mother my inner child more compassionately?

_____

_____

_____

What makes me feel safe to share my emotions and connect with my intuition?

_____

_____

_____

How can I more intentionally create spaces that make me feel safe to share my emotions and connect with my intuition?

_____

_____

_____

## Ocean Tides Healing Bath Salts

As a water sign, Cancer is linked to bodies of water of all kinds but especially the ocean. Represented by the Crab, Cancer is all about the nurturing energy of mama earth and mama ocean. Plus, Cancer is the only sign ruled by the moon, and the moon's gravitational pull regulates the ocean's tides! This recipe for homemade bath salts is perfect for adding to your new moon ritual bath in honor of our precious oceans and the magick of the sea. It's infused with the energy of the moon, the ocean, and summertime.

- 2 cups Epsom salts (for purification)
- ⅓ cup baking soda
- 8 drops eucalyptus essential oil (for healing)
- 5 drops lime essential oil (for healing)
- 3 drops angelica essential oil (for peace)

Mix the salt and baking soda together in a bowl so that they are evenly combined. Add the essential oils and mix thoroughly to combine. Scoop into a jar and store in a cool, dry place. Allow to infuse for at least a week before use. If you'd like to make this recipe right away and add the ingredients directly to your bath without prior infusion, use no more than 6 to 8 drops of essential oils total as more than this can be too intense for direct contact with skin.

The night of the new moon in Cancer (or anytime that you feel called), arrange the bathroom for your ritual. You might place moon crystals like clear quartz and moonstone on the edge of the tub, light white candles, and burn jasmine incense. One of my favorite moon rituals is a moon salutations yoga flow, to open my sacred space and move any stagnant

energy through my body. Moon salutations are like the classic sun salutations except that they're designed to relax and stretch your body rather than warm up your muscles for more rigorous exercise. Moon salutations can include flowing poses, called asanas, such as low lunge with backbend, goddess pose, child's pose, and humble warrior. You might choose to do a restorative yoga flow or moon salutation before your ritual bath.

When you're ready, fill the tub with water and pour your bath salts into the running water from the faucet so that they are carried throughout the tub. You might also hang a bundle of fresh or dried eucalyptus from the faucet for even greater healing and cleansing properties. Sink into the tub and allow your mind, body, and spirit to fully relax. Sipping on tea or moonwater (or a glass of wine), listening to music, or reading a book are all highly encouraged—self-care, baby!

## FULL MOON IN CAPRICORN

The full moon in Capricorn is a reminder that you need both structure and support in order to have experiences that are emotionally and practically sustainable. Where Cancer is all intuition and sensitivity, Capricorn is grounded in integrity. This full moon is the perfect time to reflect on and be honest with yourself about where you need more structure, accountability, and boundaries.

Am I struggling to hold myself accountable in any areas of my life?

_____

_____

_____

How can structure and boundaries be supportive and compassionate?

_____

_____

_____

What does it look like for self-care to be sustainable long-term?

_____

_____

_____

## Full Moon Anointing Oil for Grounding

Practicing grounding is such an important part of magickal and self-care workings of all kinds. Being grounded means being in touch with the earth, in tune with your body, and rooted in the practical realities of life without sacrificing the mysteries and magick of the unknown (as always, balance is essential).

As an earth sign, Capricorn is one of the most grounded energies in the zodiac, so the full moon in Capricorn is a great opportunity to do some grounding work. You can practice grounding in lots of different ways including breathwork, visualization, physical touch, walking barefoot on the earth, and many more. Anointing yourself with oils is another good option, as you are physically touching yourself and becoming aware of your physical being. Getting grounded for you might look and feel different than it does for others, as it's a very personal experience.

- 2 teaspoons carrier oil
- 3 drops cedarwood essential oil (for purification and grounding)

- 2 drops pine essential oil (for grounding)
- 2 drops cypress essential oil (for emotional support)

Combine all ingredients in a glass vial fitted with a roller ball or in a small bowl. Find a comfortable seat, perhaps under the full moon's light, if possible, and close your eyes. Drop your shoulders down your back and relax your jaw. Take a deep breath in through your nose and sigh it out through your mouth. You might repeat for a few more deep breaths or do some more structured breathwork if it feels right. Visualize a root beginning to grow out of the base of your spine. It grows down through the floor, through layers of concrete, wood, or anything else that exists between you and the earth. When it does reach the earth, the root grows down into the soil, plunging deeper and deeper in search of nutrients. As your root grows down into the earth, anchoring you, it begins to draw glowing, green, earth energy up into your body and your spirit, nourishing you.

When you feel sufficiently anchored and supported, dip your fingertips into the bowl of oil and anoint your sternum, the center of your being. Speak out loud or to yourself, "I am rooted." Dip your fingertips into the bowl again and anoint each of your knees or feet, your connection to the ground. Speak out loud or to yourself, "I am supported." Dip your fingertips into the bowl once more and anoint your third eye, the space between and just above your eyebrows, which is a channel for your intuition and higher self. Speak out loud or to yourself, "I am uplifted."

You might take this opportunity to meditate, to draw in more nourishing earth energy through your roots, or to do some journaling, chanting, or simply relaxing. When you feel complete, visualize the root growing back up through the soil and into your body, unlinking you but not disconnecting you from the earth's support. Afterward, you might do some earthing, walking barefoot on the ground, or fuel your body with healthy, nutritious foods.

# LEO SEASON (LATE JULY TO AUGUST)

Leo season is from approximately July 20 to August 19 each year, though it can shift a few days in either direction. Leo is a bold, creative, expressive sign that's all about having pride in who you are. During Leo season, you might feel bolder and more vibrant than usual. This is the season of self-love and creative self-expression, the perfect opportunity to find what brings you pure joy and lights you up. Don't hold back!

- **Dates:** July 20–August 19
- **Season:** Summer
- **Element:** Fire
- **Modality:** Fixed
- **Symbol:** The Lion
- **Archetype:** The Sovereign
- **Ruling Planet:** Sun
- **Body Part:** Heart, spine, upper back, hair
- **Tarot Card:** Strength, The Sun
- **Color:** Gold
- **Goddesses:** Inanna (Sumerian goddess of war, love, and the underworld), Amaterasu (Japanese goddess of the sun)
- **Plants:** Calendula, sunflower, cinnamon, chamomile
- **Crystals:** Sunstone, amber

Note: *The above information is for the Northern Hemisphere. In the Southern Hemisphere, Leo season, the new moon in Leo, and the full moon in Aquarius still occur in July and August but sustain us through the winter season instead of summer. Refer to the Aquarius season section for correspondences, recipes, and rituals.*

# LAMMAS

Lammas, also known as Lughnasadh, is the first of three harvest festivals. What I love about this sabbat is its subtlety; if you turn your awareness to nature at this time of year, you'll start to notice wheat and grains coming ready for harvest and dropping seeds, even the very first leaves beginning to turn yellow. Lammas is the quiet harbinger of the oncoming witch's season and an opportunity to celebrate the abundance of the year while we're still in the midst of it.

What abundance have I already manifested into my life so far this year?

_____

_____

_____

When I turn my awareness and intuition to the earth, what subtle signs of fall do I already see?

_____

_____

_____

What am I celebrating and giving thanks for?

_____

_____

_____

## Herbed Honey Butter

Lammas is often celebrated with loaves of fresh wheat- or corn-bread, to honor the summer harvest of grains and vegetables. There's little better than a slice of warm, freshly baked bread (but a slathering of honey or butter makes it even more delicious)! This recipe kicks it up a notch by combining honey *and* butter, as well as some fresh summer herbs. I've made this recipe many times over for Lammas along with a pan of corn bread and perhaps a summery meal of barbecued chicken, corn on the cob, and grilled nectarines. It never disappoints—something about the sweet, salty, herbaceous combination of flavors makes for a particularly nostalgic bite.

- fresh sage leaves (for purification)
- fresh rosemary (for healing)
- fresh thyme (for courage)

- ½ cup salted butter
- ¼ cup local honey

Destem the herbs and finely chop the leaves. Soften the butter on the stove or in the microwave for a few seconds, just until it is soft to the touch. Combine the honey, butter, and chopped herbs in a small bowl. It is best served at room temperature, so if you need to refrigerate it, let it warm up again before serving. Serve on warm slices of bread or corn bread or even on grilled corn on the cob.

As you break bread and enjoy it with this delicious salty sweet treat, whether alone or celebrating with friends or ancestors, give thanks and gratitude to the earth that nurtured these plants, to the sun that shone down and inspired them, to the rains that nourished them, to the cows that gave their milk, and to the bees that gave their honey. All of these cycles and creatures give generously of their resources so that we may enjoy abundance and bliss. You might consider making an offering of a piece of bread topped with this honey butter to the earth, the sun, or your ancestors in thanks for their generosity.

## Late Summer Harvest Sangria

Sangria is one of those refreshing summer beverages that is perfect for celebrating special occasions or simply sipping in the backyard on a warm afternoon—delightful under all circumstances. Sangria can be made with either red or white wine and just about any fruits of your choosing. This particular recipe is concentrated on the late summer berries and stone fruits that are prevalent at Lammas and during Leo season. I love working with plants that are both in season and aligned with the cosmic energies!

- 2 cups fresh blackberries (for wealth)
- 2 nectarines (for abundance)
- handful fresh thyme (for continued good health)
- 1 bottle white wine such as sauvignon blanc
- 1 cup brandy (optional)

Rinse and pat dry the blackberries and place them in a glass pitcher. Slice the nectarines and add to the pitcher. Rinse and dry the thyme and add the full stems to the pitcher. Pour the entire bottle of wine into the pitcher and top with the brandy, if desired. Stir gently with a wooden spoon and chill. Serve over ice. When you are ready to enjoy this delicious summer treat, pour yourself a glass and top with a sprig of fresh thyme.

A core theme of Leo season and Lammas is celebration. Leo is the only sign in the zodiac ruled by the sun, the luminary of joy, fun, play, and happiness. In your chart, your sun indicates what brings you the most joy and what makes you feel like a little kid again. During Leo season, we are called to celebrate those things that bring us joy, so connecting with friends and enjoying a delicious meal with a refreshing pitcher of sangria is the perfect ritual for Leo season and Lammas!

## Wheat Wreath for Abundance

Decorating with wheat is a classic symbol of Lammas, as it is one of the most sacred plants of this sabbat. Wheat symbolizes abundance, as a good harvest of wheat in late summer had a profound impact on our ancestors' ability to survive and thrive throughout the cold, barren winter months. Wheat crafts are versatile and accessible for witches of all abilities and ages and can really bring some of that abundant, grateful energy of the season into your home and altar. This wheat wreath is simple to make and will last for years.

- wire cutters
- 5–6 bundles dry wheat (for abundance)
- floral wire
- metal wreath form

With your wire cutters, cut all the wheat to about six inches in length. Create small bundles of wheat with 10 to 15 stems in each and wrap them tightly with the floral wire. Lay each bundle along the metal wreath form at a 45-degree angle and secure it tightly with more wire. Lay each bundle alongside the next, overlapping as you go until the entire wreath form is covered with overlapping bundles of wheat.

When you are satisfied with your completed wreath, it is the perfect tool to accompany a house or altar blessing ritual! You can perform this ritual at your altar or at your front door (or anywhere else you want to hang the wreath). Light white, yellow, and/or orange candles and set the space for ritual. You might burn some incense, diffuse essential oils, or cast a sacred circle. Sit in a comfortable position in front of the space where you intend to hang the wreath and place one unlit candle in front of you. Close your eyes and take a few deep breaths, clearing your energy.

Lift the unlit candle in front of you and face to the north. Speak out loud or to yourself, "I ask for the grounded protection of the earth spirits of the north." Turn to your right and face the east. Speak out loud or to yourself, "I ask for the levity and clarity of the air spirits of the east." Turn to your right and face the south. Speak out loud or to yourself, "I ask for the passionate inspiration of the fire spirits of the south." Turn to your right and face the west. Speak out loud or to yourself, "I ask for the emotional intelligence of the water spirits of the west."

Turn to your right, facing the north once more, and place the candle down in front of you again. Light the candle and hang the wreath in the location of your choosing. Take this opportunity to meditate and commune with the elemental spirits you've called in to protect and infuse your home and/or sacred space. When you feel complete, extinguish the candle, say thank you and goodbye to the spirits you've called in, and close your sacred space or circle if you have cast one.

# NEW MOON IN LEO

The new moon in Leo is a time for play, fun, and joyful self-expression. Leo is known for being bold and dramatic, so this majestic season asks you to step into your fullest expression of who you truly are with pride. Consider setting intentions this new moon around expressing your creativity and more boldly claiming your place as sovereign of your life.

In what area of my life do I need to be more authentically and boldly myself?

_____

_____

_____

How can I express my creativity more vibrantly this month?

_____

_____

_____

How is my inner sovereign going to help me feel good in my own skin?

_____

_____

_____

## Hair Oil for Nourishing Your Lion's Mane

Although Leo is best known for ruling the heart, guess what else it rules? Your glorious, lustrous (lion's) mane of hair! No matter how much hair you have, Leo rules your locks. Nourishing your hair is a way of paying tribute to your soul and your personal power and of honoring your identity and cultural expression. This hair oil is designed to nourish your hair to make it both soft and strong, so you can shine like the lioness you are.

- ¼ cup coconut oil
- ¼ cup jojoba oil
- 3–5 drops lavender oil (for softness)
- 3–5 drops cedarwood oil (for strength)
- 3–5 drops geranium oil (for fertility and growth)

Place all ingredients in a glass jar with a dropper and shake to combine. Use this oil before showering to make your entire shower experience into a Leo new moon (or anytime) self-care ritual. Set your bathroom up to become a sacred space. Clear off the countertops and tidy up so that your space feels distraction-free, if possible. Light some candles, maybe burn some incense or diffuse essential oils. Squeeze a quarter-sized amount of oil into your palm or directly onto your scalp. Massage it into your scalp, working it down toward the ends of your hair. As you apply the oil, imagine that vibrant orange energy is coating your hair, sinking into your scalp, and moving down into your body, lighting you up and empowering you. Imagine it flowing down through your head, over your shoulders, into your arms, hands, and fingers, then into your heart. From your heart, imagine this energy flowing into the rest of your body, your abdomen, your pelvis, and down into your legs and feet until your entire body is humming.

When you feel complete and alight, pin your hair up and step into the shower. As you stand under the warm water, focus your attention on the alive, empowering feeling glowing within you. When you are otherwise finished with your shower, unpin your hair and shampoo as you normally would, washing the oil away. Stand under the hot water for a few moments longer, imagining this energy fading away and withdrawing into your heart space until only your heart is left glowing. Place your hand over your heart and thank the oils and the energy for helping you tap into your own power.

## FULL MOON IN AQUARIUS

The full moon in Aquarius is a reminder that expressing your individuality is not at the expense of the collective. While Leo is the ruler of the jungle, Aquarius is the rebel leader fighting for equality for all creatures. This full moon is the perfect time to reflect on how your individual gifts and talents can be put to use for the good of your community.

How can I use my own gifts to uplift and support my community?

_____

_____

_____

Where do I feel a desire to rebel against society or even against my own rules?

_____

_____

_____

How does celebrating my own individuality benefit the collective?

_____

_____

_____

## Luminary Tea Blend for Community Support

The full moon in Aquarius is an interesting balance of energies, as the moon is at the peak of its cycle in the full moon phase in the season when the sun is in its home sign of Leo. The sun and moon do not need to vie for attention, though, as they are content to shine equally and brilliantly. As our astrological luminaries, the sun and moon are essential for supporting our inner and outer selves both individually and collectively. This tea blend is designed to be enjoyed in community—in person, if possible, or virtually over a video call (as digital technology is ruled by Aquarius), or in spirit. Have a full moon tea party and watch the moonrise together with your community and/or coven, supporting and uplifting one another.

- 2 parts dried calendula flowers (for psychic connection)
- 1 part dried lavender flowers (for love and happiness)
- 1 part dried meadowsweet (for holding space)
- 1 part oat tops (for collective prosperity)
- 2 parts oolong tea leaves (for reflection and wisdom)

Combine all ingredients except the oolong tea leaves in a glass jar and cover with boiled water. Loosely place a lid on the jar and allow to steep overnight or for at least 6 hours. Strain and place the herbal oat water in a pot on the stove, gently reheating it on medium-low heat. Fill a tea infuser or tea bag with the oolong tea leaves and place in a teapot (or mug, if making a single cup). Pour the hot herbal oat water over the infuser and allow to steep for 1 to 5 minutes.

Light five candles in a circle on a round table or the ground, preferably outside or by a window through which you can watch the moon rise. Place the teapot in the center of the candles and invite your community or coven members to join you in sitting around the table. As you sip your tea together, take this opportunity to genuinely check in, creating space for each person to share what's on their heart, what support they need, what they're grateful for, and what they're celebrating. Watch the moon rise together as you celebrate and uplift one another.

## VIRGO SEASON (LATE AUGUST TO SEPTEMBER)

Virgo season is from approximately August 20 to September 19 each year, though it can shift a few days in either direction. Virgo is a fastidious, detail-oriented sign that bridges the gap between the mundane and the spiritual through grounded rituals. If you've ever gotten excited over a new pencil case or set of pens, this season is for you. Virgo season is a great time to reevaluate your daily rituals and make adjustments if they aren't fully serving your needs.

- **Dates:** August 20–September 19
- **Season:** Summer
- **Element:** Earth

- **Modality:** Mutable
- **Symbol:** The Virgin
- **Archetype:** The Priestess
- **Ruling Planet:** Mercury (traditional) or asteroid Vesta (progressive—named for Roman goddess of the hearth and sacred flame)
- **Body Part:** Gut, intestines
- **Tarot Card:** The Hermit, The High Priestess
- **Color:** Green
- **Goddesses:** Astraea (Greek goddess of innocence and justice), Shala (Sumerian goddess of grain and compassion)
- **Plants:** Thyme, marjoram, clover, fern, fennel
- **Crystals:** Moss agate, green calcite

Note: *The above information is for the Northern Hemisphere. In the Southern Hemisphere, Virgo season, the new moon in Virgo, and the full moon in Pisces still occur in August and September but lead us through the transition from winter to spring, instead of from summer to autumn. Refer to the Pisces season section for correspondences, recipes, and rituals.*

# TRANSITION FROM SUMMER TO AUTUMN

Virgo season is the liminal space between summer and fall, as we transition from the growing season to the harvest. It's also back-to-school season for much of the world, when many of us feel a burst of new motivation and inspiration to refresh our routines, schedules, cabinets, and even our rituals. In fact, one of my favorite parts about Virgo season is the opportunity to align with our inner priestess, priest, or priestexx, and create or refresh the rituals that serve to ground our spirit in the tangible realm and to connect our mind and body with our intuitive wisdom.

How does the back-to-school vibe of late summer and early fall make me feel?

_____

_____

_____

What do I need to refresh in my daily life, routines, and rituals in order to feel truly fulfilled?

_____

_____

_____

Are there any practical steps I need to take to call in my manifestations right now?

_____

_____

_____

## Iced Blackberry Lime Mint Tea

Virgo season is the transition from summer to autumn, from the peak of the sun's power into the witch's season. Perhaps it's my own relationship to Virgo season as a Virgo rising myself, but this time of year always feels like I'm transitioning from who I have been to who I will become. This recipe capitalizes on the last of summer's sunshine and abundance to put a new twist on classic mint tea. Mint tea is best known for its delightful, aerated Moroccan presentation. Moroccan mint tea, which is actually Chinese gunpowder green tea steeped with spearmint, is typically served by pouring it into embellished glasses from a height of 1 to 2 feet.

The Dutch version of mint tea, which is closer to the inspiration for this recipe, features a handful of fresh mint in a glass with hot water poured over it. It's delightfully fresh, invigorating, and the perfect late summer beverage.

- 12–15 fresh blackberries (for healing reflection)
- 2–3 cups fresh mint on the stem (for clarity)
- 3–4 cups distilled water at room temperature
- 2 fresh limes (for inspiration)

Rinse the blackberries and pat them dry. Place one blackberry in each cup of an empty ice cube tray, cover with water, and freeze. Rinse the fresh mint and pat dry, then add to a pitcher. Cover with the distilled water until mint stems are completely submerged and place outside in the sunshine to steep. When the mint tea has reached your desired strength, bring it inside. Strain the tea and remove the mint stems or leave them submerged if you prefer. Halve the limes and squeeze the juice into the mint tea, stirring to combine. When you are ready to serve, place blackberry ice cubes in tall glasses or goblets and top with your mint tea. Garnish with a wedge of lime and enjoy in the late summer sunshine.

## Sacred Space Diffuser Blend for Daily Rituals

As the archetype of the Priestess, Virgo has a lot to do with sacredness and devotion—what you are devoted to, how you express your devotion, and what is most sacred and holy in your life. Sometimes these can be very difficult questions to answer, though. In fact, as I described in my first book, *The Modern Witch's Guide to Magickal Self-Care*, I consider devotion to be one of the pillars of a witch's spiritual practice. Yet, I often hear from people that they find answering this question of "what are you devoted to?" a bigger challenge to answer than they had hoped! It's not that we aren't devoted to people, things, and ideas, but it's not very often that we're asked to put those ideas into words and to describe how we express that devotion. The more you know what you're truly devoted to, the more intentional you can be about how you use your time, energy, and resources to express that devotion.

This diffuser blend is designed for two purposes. First, it's great for creating sacred space wherever you are and for cleansing your space prior to ritual. However, it's also great for when you feel out of sync with your devotion and with what is sacred to you, to help you realign with whatever it is that matters most in your reality.

- 3 drops vetiver essential oil (for banishing ill will)
- 3 drops patchouli essential oil (for ritual consecration)
- 2 drops sandalwood essential oil (for high spiritual vibrations)

Combine all ingredients in water in an ultrasonic diffuser or in a reed diffuser and allow the grounding, herbaceous, and musky scents to infuse your space. If using this diffuser to open sacred space before a ritual (such as your daily morning or evening ritual, a moon ritual, or a ritual for self-care or spellwork), place the diffuser on your altar or in the space where you plan to perform your ritual. Take your time filling the diffuser with water and placing the oils in it.

Turn the diffuser on and find a comfortable seat, perhaps cross-legged or with your feet flat on the ground. Close your eyes if it feels safe and right to do so and take three deep breaths, in through your nose and out through your mouth. Imagine that there is a glowing golden sphere surrounding you, like a bubble. Imagine the scent from the diffuser flowing up and up until it reaches the top of the sphere, then filling the entire bubble, flowing down the sides and all around you. When the bubble is filled with this cleansing scent, your sacred space is open. To close your sacred space, thank the herbs that the oils were distilled from for their support in lifting the vibration and consecrating your space, then turn off the diffuser.

## Crystal & Herb Grid for Sacred Space

Crystal grids are a fun way to work with the tools of nature to create sacred space and direct your energy toward a specific goal or outcome. A crystal grid is simply a geometric and symmetrical grid formed with crystals and sometimes other materials such as fresh herbs. This grid incorporates both crystals and fresh herbs to help you bless and dedicate your altar or another sacred space. Altars are essentially a flat surface that is dedicated to and decorated in honor of your spiritual beliefs, ancestors, deities, or a cosmic cycle or entity such as the seasons or moon phases. An altar can include just about any object that feels sacred and special to you. They can be very elaborate and obvious or very small and subtle.

This grid includes crystals that are great for grounding and that heal by helping you tap into your innate connection to the earth. It also includes one of the most cleansing crystals, selenite, which actually absorbs and dissolves negative energy, as well as fresh thyme, one of the most sacred Virgo herbs. If you don't have some or all of these crystals, you can always substitute clear quartz, which has a neutral energy that you can program with your desired intention.

- 6 small moss agate crystals (for healing)
- 4 small aragonite crystals (for grounding)

- 6 stems fresh thyme (for sacredness)
- 1 medium or large selenite crystal (for cleansing)

Place the crystals outside or in a windowsill to cleanse in moonlight or cleanse them with burning sage or cedar smoke. Hold the moss agate crystals together in your cupped palms. Ask your deity or spirit to bless them or simply focus on your intention to create a sacred space. Place the moss agate crystals in a circle on your altar, evenly spaced. Hold the aragonite crystals in your cupped palms and ask for a blessing or focus on your intention. Place the aragonite in an evenly spaced square inside the circle of moss agate crystals. Hold the stems of fresh thyme in your hands and ask for a blessing or focus on your intention. Lay one stem between each of the moss agate crystals, pointing into the center of the grid. Hold the selenite crystal in your cupped palms and ask for a blessing or focus on your intention. Reverently, place the crystal in the center of your grid to complete it.

Leave the crystal and herb grid until the herbs are dry and its work of creating sacred space and consecrating your altar feels complete. When you are ready to take apart your grid, do so with great reverence and remove each item in the same order that you laid it down. Dispose of the dried herbs outside of your home.

## NEW MOON IN VIRGO

The new moon in Virgo is a time for checking in and realigning with your rituals and routines. Virgo energy has a gift for making the mundane feel magickal, as well as for using ritual and spirituality to nourish your physical health and wellness. Consider setting intentions this new moon around refreshing your daily rituals.

How well are my daily rituals currently serving me?

_____

_____

_____


How do I want my daily rituals and routines to feel, compared to how they currently feel?

_____

_____

_____


What wisdom does my inner priestess have for me around creating rituals that are fulfilling and useful?

_____

_____

_____


## Priestess Candle Dressing Blend

This candle dressing oil is designed to help you channel your inner priestess, but being a priestess is not just about lighting sacred flames in ancient temples! The role of a priestess is to facilitate connection between the physical world and the spiritual, mystical, metaphysical realm beyond. That might sound elaborate and esoteric, but the truth is, every time you perform a ritual—even the most mundane of routines to care for your health and wellness—you are acting as a priestess, priest, or priestexx. This oil blend will help you create a magickal talisman in the form of a dressed candle that can create sacred space and help put you in the mindset for spiritual experiences anywhere you go.

- 2 teaspoons carrier oil such as sunflower or olive oil
- 2–3 drops frankincense essential oil (for spiritual protection)
- 2–3 drops cedarwood essential oil (for purification and intuitive clarity)
- 1–2 drops clove essential oil (for high spiritual vibrations)

Combine all the oils in a small bowl, mixing them gently. Alternatively, you could combine them in a bottle fitted with a roller ball cap. Take a white birthday or chime candle and hold it in one hand. Dip your fingers in the oil mixture and rub the oil onto the candle, starting from the bottom and working your way up to the middle, then from the top down to the middle. If using a roller ball bottle, simply roll the oil onto the candle from bottom to middle and top to middle. Rubbing the oil into the center of the candle is to call in energy, as opposed to banishing it.

Place the candle in a fire-safe holder and strike a match. As you light the candle, say out loud or silently to yourself, "I consecrate this space

and time as sacred and devote it to [your choice of devotional]." You could devote your ritual to a god or goddess, to your ancestors, to your own self-care, to connecting with your intuition, or to any other spiritual pursuit.

If devoting your ritual and candle to a goddess, you might want to add 1 to 2 drops of an additional oil to specifically align with her energy. If you do choose to dedicate your candle to a particular goddess, you should plan to only light it when working with her. Here are some suggestions of oils to work with for popular goddesses:

- **Aphrodite/Venus (Greco-Roman):** Rose essential oil (for opening the heart)
- **Artemis/Diana (Greco-Roman):** Sage essential oil (for purification)
- **Athena/Minerva (Greco-Roman):** Black pepper essential oil (for action)
- **Brigid (Celtic):** Chamomile essential oil for (healing and dreams)
- **Demeter/Ceres (Greco-Roman):** Sandalwood essential oil (for peace, strength, and renewal)
- **Freya (Norse):** Rose hip carrier oil (for love and psychic ability)
- **Hekate (Greek):** Cypress essential oil (for healing and releasing)
- **Inanna (Sumerian):** Fir essential oil (for renewal)
- **Lakshmi (Hindu):** Basil essential oil (for fertility and desire)
- **Persephone/Proserpina (Greco-Roman):** Pomegranate carrier oil (for connecting with the underworld)

## FULL MOON IN PISCES

The full moon in Pisces is a reminder that it's okay to tap deeply into the mystical and the spiritual and that not everything needs to be practical.

Where Virgo is hyper-focused on bridging the gap between the practical and the spiritual, Pisces goes all in with the intuitive, empathic, mystical energy. This full moon is perfect for divination, dream work, spirit guide journeying, and ritual baths.

In what ways does my intuition speak through me most clearly?

_____

_____

_____

How can I trust my intuition more deeply?

_____

_____

_____

What message does my intuition have for me?

_____

_____

_____

## Bath Tea for Nourishing Intuition

Bath teas, also known as tub teas, are blends of herbs and oils meant to infuse bathtub water with their healing and magickal properties. They're like a delightful cross between bath oils and potpourri and are perfect for your next ritual bath. Ritual baths, in turn, are perfect for the full moon in Pisces, one of the most intuitive moon phases of the year. This bath tea is designed to help nourish your intuition so that you can connect with your inner oracle and channel messages from the divine, your spirit guides, or your higher self, especially when paired with the special ritual bath below.

- 5–8 drops neroli* essential oil (for communicating with the spirit realm)
- ½ cup dried lavender flowers (for intuition)
- ½ cup dried jasmine flowers (for prophetic dreams)
- ¼ cup dried bladderwrack seaweed or kelp (for psychic ability)

Add the essential oil directly to the dried ingredients and stir to combine. Scoop the bath tea into a muslin bag and tie securely shut. When ready to use, place the muslin bag over the faucet of the tub so that the hot water runs through it into the bath. You can also submerge the bag directly in the hot water.

Arrange the bathroom for your ritual with white, blue, or purple candles, and crystals such as amethyst, fluorite, and clear quartz. I also recommend playing some soft music or, even better, recordings of ocean waves. You might also burn some cleansing incense or a smoke bundle and wave it over yourself before undressing to purify your aura and energy. Fill the bathtub and rest your body in the soothing, warm water. Cup the water in your hands and pour it over your body, inhaling the sweet, cleansing scent of the bath tea. Place your fingertips on your third eye, the space just between and slightly above your eyebrows, closing your eyes if it feels right. Feel your mind begin to expand, taking in all the sensory information around you. Notice what you hear, feel, smell, and

---

* You can substitute grapefruit essential oil for neroli oil if you prefer, as neroli oil can be quite expensive.

taste. Then, allow your mind and intuition to drift further, outside of the physical senses and experiences around you. You might imagine yourself floating deep underwater in the sea or drifting through the vastness of space. Release control of the visualization and allow yourself to be guided wherever you need to go and to whatever guides or messages you need to receive. When you feel your journey is complete, open your eyes and slowly come back into your body. You might choose to journal or pull tarot or oracle cards to clarify the messages you received.

# Chapter 6

# AUTUMN

Autumn is the witch's season, the most magickal time of the year, when the veil between worlds is said to be at its thinnest. This time of year is aligned with the Crone aspect of the Triple Goddess. Autumn is known for abundant harvests and giving gratitude, for brilliant colors of red and orange, and for the first crisp, cold days. Energetically, autumn is aligned with the element of water. It's a foggy morning that gives way to afternoon apple picking and evening bonfires.

In terms of the seasonal, lunar, and astrological cycles, autumn in the Northern Hemisphere is home to:

- Libra season, which begins at the autumn equinox, and includes the Libra new moon and Aries full moon.
- Scorpio season, which includes the festival of Samhain, the Scorpio new moon, and Taurus full moon.
- Sagittarius season, which leads us through the transition to winter and includes the Sagittarius new moon and Gemini full moon.

On the following pages, I'm going to share correspondences and recipes to help you embody and be in flow with all of these festivals, lunations, and seasonal rhythms!

Note: *In the Southern Hemisphere, Libra, Scorpio, and Sagittarius seasons occur during autumn. If you live south of the equator, refer to the sections on the opposite signs, Aries, Taurus, and Gemini, for inspiration on celebrating these seasons.*

# LIBRA SEASON (LATE SEPTEMBER TO OCTOBER)

Libra season is from approximately September 20 to October 19 each year, though it can shift a few days in either direction. Libra is a social, creative, fair-minded sign that's all about the way we relate to one another. During Libra season, you may find that you're suddenly all about interpersonal connections and collaborations. There might be a bit of romance in the air, or you might just feel really connected with your closest friends, siblings, and business partners. There's also an energy of fairness and equality here so some social justice action may be in the cards.

- **Dates:** September 20–October 19
- **Season:** Autumn
- **Element:** Air
- **Modality:** Cardinal
- **Symbol:** The Scales
- **Archetype:** The Lover
- **Ruling Planet:** Venus (traditional) or asteroid Juno (progressive—named for Roman goddess of marriage)
- **Body Part:** Lower back, buttocks
- **Tarot Card:** Justice, The Empress
- **Color:** Pink
- **Goddesses:** Maat (Egyptian goddess of harmony, justice, and truth), Radha (Hindu goddess of love and tenderness)

- **Plants:** Cardamom, hyacinth, lilac, rose, elder
- **Crystals:** Rose quartz, ametrine

*The above information is for the Northern Hemisphere. In the Southern Hemisphere, Libra season, the new moon in Libra, and the full moon in Aries still occur in September and October but herald the beginning of the spring season instead of autumn. Refer to the Aries season section for correspondences, recipes, and rituals.*

# AUTUMN EQUINOX

The autumn equinox is one of the two days of the entire year when daylight and nighttime hours are equal and balanced. It's the second harvest festival, a time of feasting, gathering, and gratitude. This is an excellent time to gather for a "Friendsgiving" celebration of sorts and break bread with the people you love. In fact, sharing and genuinely connecting with your loved ones is aligned with the energy of both the autumn equinox and Libra season itself.

How can I express gratitude in a meaningful and heart-centered way?

_____

_____

_____

Why do we gather to feast and share conversation with the people we love?

_____

_____

_____

How can I share with others the abundance I have, whatever form it takes on?

_____

_____

_____

## Botanical Gin

Several years ago, my parents gave me and my roommate a kit for making our own gin. They knew it was the perfect gift for us. We'd get to mess with plants and herbs, then end up with some delicious gin to add to our home bar (which was already fairly extensive). And they were right—we had so much fun with the original kit that we saved the recipe so we could make it again and again! We've made it for ourselves many times and to give as gifts.

Now, this is a bit of a cheater recipe as you're starting with vodka, not fermenting the alcohol from scratch, but it is very easy, fun, and satisfying. This botanical gin is great for celebrating the autumn equinox, as it's the perfect (semi)-homemade contribution to the Witch's Friendsgiving feast and it includes plants you can harvest from your own yard or easily pick up at the grocery store. You can mix and match just about any herbs, dried fruits, or flowers that you'd like to include.

- ¼ cup dried juniper berries (for releasing outcomes)
- 16 ounces mid-quality plain vodka
- ½–1 cup fresh herbs and spices of your choice such as rosemary, thyme, lavender, coriander, orange or lemon peel, cardamom, clove, star anise, angelica, peppercorns, or cinnamon

Place the juniper berries in the bottom of a glass bottle and pour the vodka over them. Seal tightly with a lid or cork and store in a cool, dry place for 12 to 24 hours. Open the bottle and add the herbs and spices of your choosing. Seal tightly again and store in a cool, dry place for 24 to 36 hours more. Pour the gin through a fine-mesh strainer into a bowl, then use a funnel to pour the strained liquid back into the bottle.

Enjoy over ice or in a cocktail for your autumn equinox feast or anytime! If you're hosting or attending an equinox gathering, your homemade gin is perfect for a gratitude toast to kick off the festivities.

### Festive Harvest Cocktail
### (per serving)

- 2 ounces homemade botanical gin (for gratitude)
- 5 ounces sparkling apple cider (for magick)
- Before you sit down to enjoy your feast, have everyone raise a glass of this delicious drink (or of a glass of sparkling cider for a nonalcoholic option), and share what they're grateful for.

## Gratitude Diffuser Blend

I love to use my essential oil diffuser all year long, but I find myself employing it most as the autumn equinox rolls around. There's just something so comforting and cozy about the sweet, spicy scents of the fall season! Cinnamon, clove, ginger, and cedar—I love them all.

This diffuser blend is designed to inspire gratitude. Gratitude is one of those buzzy words that we throw around a lot in the spiritual community, but it really does hold so much value. I used to have a hard time with gratitude because it felt like something that we go through the motions of but don't necessarily really embody. It seems like every manifesting influencer and self-care journal tells you to write down what you're grateful for every day. I felt silly doing that for a long time but when I finally decided to start a real gratitude practice and to dedicate time to it every day just to see what would happen . . . I was floored by the results.

I started writing down five things I was grateful for each morning in my journal—some material things, some in-the-moment experiences like being grateful for the weather that day, and some bigger, more soul-level gratitudes. And these small acts of focusing my attention on the gratitude I felt for being able to live the life I want and receive the abundance I desire, even just for a few moments a day, snowballed and multiplied like I never could have imagined. It's not lip service or a phony ritual (even if it feels a little silly at first), I promise!

- 3 drops cinnamon essential oil (for success)
- 3 drops nutmeg essential oil (for abundance)
- 2 drops juniper essential oil (for gratitude)

Diffuse this blend when working with gratitude practices or rituals. You might diffuse it on your bedside table while doing some gratitude journaling in the morning or during your workday to help inspire gratitude in your regular, daily life. You can also diffuse it during your autumn equinox gathering to inspire grateful hearts in everyone!

If you're new to gratitude practices, consider building a gratitude ritual around this recipe. Each morning, set aside 5 to 10 minutes for your ritual. Light some candles, put on some music, whatever you need to feel aligned and relaxed, and set your diffuser. Sit on your bed, in a comfortable chair, or on a meditation pillow with your journal and a pen in your lap. Close your eyes and take a few deep breaths to center yourself and arrive in this moment. When you feel ready, open your journal and write down at least five things you're grateful for and why you're grateful for them. How do they enrich and brighten your life? If you feel called to write down more than five, do it! I also encourage you to review your gratitude journal at least once a month. You'll be amazed by how much abundance you have in your life, even on days when it feels out of reach.

## Pressed Leaves

Pressed leaves are perfect for preserving a little bit of autumn and bringing some fresh, fall color into your home.

- colorful fall leaves (especially maple or other large, flat, pointed leaves)
- wax paper
- heavy book

Select colorful leaves that have already fallen from trees on your property or out in nature. If you really feel called to select leaves still attached to a tree, consider leaving an offering or asking for the tree's permission first. Cut a piece of wax paper and open a heavy book to a center page. Fold the wax paper in half and lay it open inside the book. Place your leaves on the right side of the wax paper. Carefully close the book over the leaves, being sure that they stay flat between the piece of wax paper. Press down firmly on the book, then place it in a safe location where it can remain undisturbed for a week or up to 2 to 3 weeks. After a week, check on the leaves to see if they are sufficiently dried and flattened. If not, allow to press for another 1 to 2 weeks.

Once the leaves are dried, you can make them into a garland, press them into your grimoire, or use them for fall decoration. You can even turn them into placemats for your Friendsgiving feast by simply gluing or double stick taping the leaves to 12" x 18" sheets of white or colored paper in an attractive arrangement and laminating them. This is a great fall project to do with kids or to decorate the kids table at your equinox gathering. An even easier table décor project is to write each guest's name on a pressed leaf in gold marker and place them on each plate as place settings.

## NEW MOON IN LIBRA

The new moon in Libra is a time of celebration and gratitude. As the sign of the Scales, Libra is all about balance and, not coincidentally, is also one of the signs that leads us into an equinox (when daylight and nighttime hours are balanced). Because this is the season of the autumn equinox, there is a real sense of abundance and gratitude for a successful harvest of manifestations and personal growth. Consider setting intentions at this new moon for balance, beauty, and more intimate relationships.

What am I most grateful for so far this year?

_____

_____

_____

What area of my life is most in need of greater balance and beauty?

_____

_____

_____

How does my inner lover want me to express gratitude in the context of my relationships?

_____

_____

_____

# Bath Salts for Inner & Outer Balance

The new moon in Libra is a great time to reflect on and set some intentions around how you can create more balance and harmony in your real, daily life throughout the year. It's also a great time to focus on how you can create more balance and equity in the world around you— how you can uplift those who have been marginalized or oppressed and have experienced an imbalance of opportunities, wealth, and well-being. These fragrant, floral bath salts are designed to cultivate inner balance within your heart, mind, and emotions and to open your eyes to the ways in which you can create equity around you.

- 2 cups Epsom salts
- ⅓ cup baking soda
- ½ cup dried elderflower (for healing hearts)
- ½ cup dried lavender flowers (for balance)
- 5 drops cardamom essential oil (for partnership)
- 5 drops ylang-ylang essential oil (for peace)

Mix the salts and baking soda together in a bowl until they are evenly combined. Add the essential oils and mix thoroughly. Scoop into a jar and store in a cool, dry place. Allow to infuse for at least a week before use. If you'd like to make this recipe right away and add the ingredients directly to your bath without prior infusion, use no more than 6 to 8 drops of essential oils total, as more than this can be too intense for direct contact with skin.

For your new moon ritual, set the atmosphere by lighting some candles and placing crystals such as amethyst, ametrine, and rose quartz around the edge of the bath. When you're ready, fill the tub with water and pour the bath salts into the running water from the faucet so that they are carried throughout the tub. If you have a bath tray, place it across the tub or place a small table beside the tub for your journal and pen. Sink into the warm, soothing water and allow your entire body to relax. Close your eyes, relax your shoulders, and imagine that the water around you is actually the ocean or a large lake extending far out into the edges of your periphery. You are floating here peacefully, drifting across the water, perfectly balanced. The water is just the right temperature, and you can feel a gentle breeze caressing your face.

As you float, open your heart and your mind and ask for guidance on how you can create or receive greater balance and equity in your life and in the world. Float here in this peaceful meditation for as long as you like and, when you feel ready, return to your body and journal on the messages you received.

## FULL MOON IN ARIES

The full moon in Aries is a reminder not to sacrifice your sense of self in the process of deepening your relationships and giving gratitude to all the people and situations that have helped you grow. While Libra is gracious, Aries is direct and reminds you to put *you* first. This is the halfway point in the lunar year—it has been just about six months since we celebrated the new moon in Aries around the spring equinox. This is a great time to reflect on your intentions from that new moon and whether they are still in alignment, as well as to course correct your goals if need be.

Are the goals and intentions I set at the new moon in Aries still in alignment?

_____

_____

_____

If not, what can I do to realign my actions to get back on track or release them?

_____

_____

_____

How have I grown and what have I experienced in the past six months?

_____

_____

_____

## Spiced Apple Chai for the Harvest Moon

It wouldn't be autumn without my favorite apple pie and chai spices! As soon as fall rolls around, you'll find me drinking some variation on this apple chai to really celebrate the season. Chai spices are perfect for the full moon in Aries, as they embody the spirit of the autumn season as well as the fire and passion of the first sign in the zodiac.

- 3 parts Ceylon black tea (for success)
- 1 part dried apple slices or chunks (for magickal manifestations)
- spices, to taste:
  - cinnamon sticks, gently crushed (for passion)

- ◦ cardamom pods, gently crushed (for intimacy)
- ◦ black peppercorns (for protection)
- ◦ pink peppercorns (for love)
- ◦ whole nutmeg, grated (for success)
- • star anise (for luck)

Combine all ingredients in a small bowl and store in a glass jar in a cool, dry place. When ready to enjoy, scoop a tablespoon of the mixture into a tea infuser or empty tea bag and place in a mug. Pour hot water over the infuser or tea bag and allow to steep for 3 to 5 minutes.

The full moon in Aries is often the Harvest Moon, the full moon closest to the autumn equinox, and can be a brilliant golden or orange hue when it first rises. This hue has to do with the atmosphere through which we see the full moon this time of year and it is certainly beautiful! On the night of the full moon in Aries, determine where from your house or nearby you can watch the moonrise. If you can see it from your home, set yourself up with a nice pot of apple chai, some candles, and any other ritual tools you like to use on the full moon such as crystals or a journal. If you won't be able to watch the moonrise from home, find a spot nearby where you can safely watch and take a chair, blanket, and thermos of chai there to watch in wonder as the moon rises over the horizon.

## SCORPIO SEASON [LATE OCTOBER TO NOVEMBER]

Scorpio season is from approximately October 20 to November 19 each year, though it can shift a few days in either direction. Scorpio is a deeply mystical, mysterious, potent sign that's all about transformation and rising from the ashes of who we used to be. During Scorpio season, you may delve deeper into your shadows and personal underworld. This is an emotional, often intense time, when you might be receiving messages from your higher self, ancestors, and spirit guides. They're not here to frighten you, though. They're here to help you grow into your favorite version of you.

- **Dates:** October 20–November 19
- **Season:** Autumn
- **Element:** Water
- **Modality:** Fixed
- **Symbol:** The Scorpion
- **Archetype:** The Witch
- **Ruling Planet:** Pluto (named for Roman god of the underworld)
- **Body Part:** Reproductive organs, genitalia
- **Tarot Card:** Death, Queen of Swords
- **Color:** Black
- **Goddesses:** Persephone (Greek goddess of vegetation and the underworld), Lilith (Judaic demon goddess and first wife of Adam)
- **Plants:** Damiana, pomegranate, basil, nettle
- **Crystals:** Smoky quartz, obsidian

*The above information is for the Northern Hemisphere. In the Southern Hemisphere, Scorpio season, the new moon in Scorpio, and the full moon in Taurus still occur in October and November but sustain us through the spring season instead of autumn. Refer to the Taurus season section for correspondences, recipes, and rituals.*

# SAMHAIN

Samhain is said to be the most magickal day of the year, when the veil between worlds is at its thinnest and spirits, faeries, and ancestors can cross over to visit us—for benevolent, malevolent, or mischievous purposes alike. Modern Halloween festivities are rooted in ancient Celtic customs designed to allow our ancestors and the supernatural to pass among us for this one night of the year. It's an excellent time for magick, divination, and shadow work of all kinds.

What shadows do I feel called to acknowledge and explore?

_____

_____

_____

Am I open to meeting with my healed and well-intentioned ancestors on the most magickal night of the year? Why or why not?

_____

_____

_____

What messages or wisdom do the spirits have for me?

_____

_____

_____

## Pomegranate Chocolate Bites

Pomegranates are associated with Samhain because they are in season in late fall but also because they are connected to the myth of Persephone, the Greek goddess of vegetation and the underworld. When Persephone was abducted by Hades (god of the underworld), her mother (Demeter, goddess of agriculture) enlisted the help of Hekate (goddess of witchcraft). Once Demeter and Hekate discovered what happened to Persephone, they petitioned Zeus (king of the gods) to help them get her back. But during her time in the underworld, Persephone had eaten six pomegranate seeds, unaware that eating anything in the underworld would trap her there forever. Zeus commanded Demeter and Hades to reach an agreement wherein Persephone would remain in the underworld with Hades for six months out of the year, reflected by the six seeds she had eaten, and return to earth to be with her mother for the remainder of the year.

The myth of Persephone explains the changing seasons. When Persephone is in the underworld with her husband throughout fall and winter, all the crops wither and die because Demeter is grieving the loss of her daughter. Many witches work with pomegranates at Samhain to honor Persephone as the queen of the underworld, with the belief that part of the reason the veil between worlds is thinnest at this time of year is because Persephone herself is in transition from the land of the living to the land of the dead.

These delicious pomegranate chocolate bites are one of my favorite treats in late fall and early winter, as they are a wildly delicious way to honor the season (and Persephone)!

- 6 ounces dark chocolate chips or chunks (for loving your own shadows)
- 2 tablespoons salted butter, optional
- seeds from 1 fresh pomegranate (for magick)
- sea salt (for purification)

Gently melt the chocolate and butter, if using, in a glass bowl in the microwave or over the stove. In the bottom of each cup of a 24-count mini muffin tin, sprinkle a layer of pomegranate seeds. Scoop a spoonful of chocolate over the pomegranates in each cup, then repeat with another layer of pomegranate seeds and another layer of chocolate. Top with a sprinkling of sea salt. Place the muffin tin in the freezer for at least 1 to 2 hours or overnight until the chocolate is set. Pop frozen chocolate bites out of the muffin tin and place in a Tupperware container to store, with wax paper sheets between layers. Keep frozen, as chocolate will melt. Enjoy with a cup of tea or glass of red wine or port!

## Candle Dressing Oil for Ancestor Veneration

When we say that the "veil between worlds is at its thinnest" in late October, what we mean is that the energetic barriers between the physical realm and the spirit realm become thin enough for spirits and messages to pass back and forth. This is reflected in the cultural traditions of Samhain on October 31 in Scotland and Dia de los Muertos on November 1 in Mexico, both celebrating the return of ancestors who have passed on. Coincidence? I think not!

Ancestor veneration, the practice of honoring and even worshipping ancestors, is a common practice in cultures all over the world. Many cultures believe that our ancestors become guides who support and guide us throughout our lives, until we too become ancestors. We have many different types of ancestors, as well: there are the people in your family tree from whom you are directly descended or by whom you were adopted, the peoples of your ancient ancestral cultures (the part of the world where your ancestors hail from), and, if you occupy an identity such as LGBTQIA2, non-binary, or even witch, there are also the social

ancestors who bravely forged a path toward acceptance and justice. Especially if the energy of your biological family feels toxic and negative or if you do not know who your biological family was, you can work with these cultural or social ancestors instead.

This candle dressing oil is designed to help you connect with and honor your ancestors, whether they be biological, adopted, cultural, or social. Connecting with your ancestors who are healed or ascended themselves, not still carrying the trauma of their lives but who are ready to support and guide you, can be a powerful way to practice ancestral healing and break generational curses or heal generational trauma. As you heal your own heart and soul, you heal your lineage, too—sending a healing ripple not only forward to your future descendants, but also back to your ancestors.

- 2 teaspoons carrier oil such as sunflower or olive oil
- 2–3 drops cypress essential oil (for honoring the dead)
- 2–3 drops rosemary essential oil (for remembering the dead)
- 1–2 drops patchouli essential oil (for communicating with spirits)

Before you dress the candle, set up an ancestor altar. You might include photographs or paintings of your ancestors (but never of living relatives or of yourself), trinkets and tokens that belonged to your ancestors, or representations of your ancestral cultures. Purify the space of negative energy by lighting cleansing incense, ringing a bell or chime, or burning common sage or cedar. Then, shield your energy and altar space by envisioning a silvery bubble of light expanding to surround your entire home.

Combine the oils in a small bowl, mixing them gently. Alternatively, you could combine them in a bottle fitted with a roller ball cap. Take a black birthday or chime candle and hold it in one hand. Dip your fingers in the oil mixture and rub the oil onto the candle, starting from the bottom and working your way up to the middle, then from the top down to the middle. If using a roller ball bottle, simply roll the oil onto the candle from bottom to middle and top to middle. Rubbing the oil into the center of the candle is to call in energy, as opposed to banishing it.

Place the candle in a fire-safe holder on your ancestor altar and strike a match. As you light the candle, say out loud or silently to yourself, "I call in my healed ancestors who have my best interests at heart. I am open to receiving your support." You might then eat a meal that originates from your ancestral culture, leaving an offering of a small portion on the altar, meditate, or pull tarot cards to receive messages from your ancestors. When your ritual feels complete, thank the spirits for joining you, ask them to return to their realm, and extinguish the candle.

## Jack-O'-Lantern Carving

Carving jack-o'-lanterns is one of my favorite Samhain or Halloween activities. It might seem basic or even childish but hear me out! The practice of carving jack-o'-lanterns actually originates in Celtic countries centuries ago, when faces were carved in turnips, parsnips, and other root vegetables on the eve of Samhain and placed in windows and doorways to ward off evil spirits. When colonizers arrived in the Americas, they discovered that indigenous squash, particularly pumpkins, were excellent for both eating and carving.

Since ancestors and spirit guides can cross over into our world on Samhain, it stands to reason that those other spirits—spirits that might wish us harm—could also cross over. That's why jack-o'-lanterns are not only a fun project, but also serve as a magickal protection spell! Every year at my house, we have a girls' night the week of Halloween to carve our pumpkins, watch witchy movies, eat snacks, and make a little magick together.

- small carving pumpkin (for abundance)
- newspaper
- steak or paring knife
- large metal spoon
- black felt-tip pen
- glass or plastic bowl
- nail polish remover

If you can, find a local pick-your-own pumpkin patch and make an early morning of it. There's nothing to set the mood like trudging through a field of pumpkins on a foggy morning to cut your own pumpkins from the vine. Otherwise, you can easily pick up a pumpkin at your local grocery store or farmers' market. Cover the table in newspaper and lay out all of your tools. To begin, cut the bottom out of your pumpkin with your steak or paring knife so that it can sit flat on the hole you've cut.

## PRO TIP

Cutting the bottom out of your pumpkin means no trying to make the top fit back on at the end, *and* you can lift it up to light the candle inside instead of reaching down into a gutted pumpkin. However, the downside is that sometimes the pumpkin will rot faster with an open bottom, so only follow this method if carving your pumpkin shortly before or on Samhain.

Use a metal spoon to scoop out the innards of your pumpkin into your glass or plastic bowl until the inside is smooth and clean. (See recipe for pumpkin seeds below.) With your black felt-tip pen, sketch a design onto the side of your pumpkin and carve it out with the knife. When you're happy with your finished design, use your nail polish remover to remove any lingering sketch marks.

Place your jack-o'-lantern in a window or outside by the front door to guard your home against spirits and bad vibes. Place a candle inside or underneath it to light up the face from within. You might even bless the candle with ancestor oil or gratitude oil! Compost the remaining innards of your pumpkin and the pumpkin itself after Samhain.

## Roasted Sweet & Spicy Pumpkin Seeds

- olive oil
- sea salt
- cinnamon (for protection)
- cayenne or chili powder (for protection)

Rinse and sort raw pumpkin seeds onto a baking sheet, removing any strings or bits of pumpkin. Combine olive oil with sea salt, cinnamon, and cayenne or chili power and sprinkle on top of seeds. Roast at 400°F for 10 to 15 minutes for a sweet and spicy snack!

# NEW MOON IN SCORPIO

Scorpio is all about the occult and witchcraft, about honoring the dead and even death itself (both literal and metaphorical). This new moon, consider setting intentions around embodying and embracing witchcraft in your life more fully and potently.

How can I embrace my inner witch more fully?

_____

_____

_____

What does it mean for me to meet my own darkness?

_____

_____

_____

How can magick and witchcraft support me over the next month?

_____

_____

_____

## Shadow Work Tea

There are very few practices that are universal among witches, but shadow work is one of them. The "shadow" is a term coined by psychologist, Carl Jung, who was actually interested in astrology and the occult himself. Shadow work is the process of acknowledging, understanding, and integrating, transmuting, or releasing the blocks, fears, shame, and limitations that we hold within us. This is essential because when we do not face our shadows, it's all too easy to carry our trauma with us into future situations and relationships and continue to inflict harm on ourselves and others. Shadow work is deeply healing and cathartic for this reason.

The new moon in Scorpio is a great time to start or boost your shadow work practice. Drink this tea anytime you need some support in facing your shadows.

- 3 parts Ceylon black tea (for confidence)
- 2 parts dried peppermint (for banishing and release)
- 2 parts dried orange peel (for self-awareness)
- 1 part dried yarrow (for spiritual protection)
- 1 part dried juniper berries (for banishing negativity)
- grated nutmeg, to taste (for strengthening determination)

Combine all ingredients in a small bowl and stir to mix. Store in a glass jar in a cool, dry place. When ready to use, scoop a tablespoon of the mixture into a tea infuser or an empty tea bag. Place the infuser or tea bag in a mug and pour hot water over it. Allow to steep for 3 to 5 minutes.

When you feel called to do shadow work, pour yourself a cup of this tea and find a quiet, secluded spot—perhaps at your altar, outside, or in a cozy, comfortable area in your house. Shadow work can be emotional, so you might want to be alone or somewhere you can receive comfort if needed. You could also light some black candles, place protective crystals like obsidian and smoky quartz around you, and do some grounding and shielding before you begin to protect your energy.

There are three essential components of shadow work:

1. **Acknowledgment:** The process of acknowledging (or admitting) that a shadow exists or that it's holding you back.
2. **Understanding:** Becoming aware of where this shadow comes from and why you currently believe it to be true.
3. **Next Steps:** You then have three options for how to proceed with your shadow work:

4. **Integration:** Deciding that this "shadow" is actually a positive thing—one of your many superpowers—and integrating it into your reality in a positive way.

5. **Transmutation:** Reframing the way you interact with this shadow and transforming it *into* a strength or superpower.

6. **Release:** Releasing this shadow and its limitations from your life.

Choose a shadow that you want to work on. This could be something you feel afraid of, ashamed about, or some kind of block or internal obstacle that you feel is holding you back from the life you truly desire. Begin by journaling on this shadow, asking yourself where it comes from, why you believe it to be a negative, and how this belief may be holding you back. Sip your tea as you journal, taking your time and pausing to rest or reflect as often as you need to. You might also want to meditate and ask your spirit guides for assistance or pull tarot or oracle cards to help you understand this shadow. When you have a deeper understanding of this shadow than you did when you began and if you feel you are ready to move forward, ask yourself whether you want to integrate, transmute, or release the shadow. It's perfectly okay, even advisable, to do this over a series of multiple sessions rather than all at once.

- **If you want to integrate the shadow:** Write down why this shadow is actually a positive power in your life and at least one or two action steps for how you will move forward. On the next new moon, reflect on these action steps and the progress you've made so far.

- **If you want to transmute the shadow:** Write down at least one negative and one positive way of seeing this shadow. Tear out the portion with the negative framing and burn it in a fire-safe container or dispose of it outside of your house. Post the positive framing somewhere you see often.

- **If you want to release the shadow:** Write down why you believe you need to release this shadow from your life and all the ways it's holding you back. Conversely, write down all the ways that releasing it will enliven and uplift your future. Tear the paper out and crumple or tear it up, then burn it in a fire-safe container or dispose of it outside of your house.

**Please note that shadow work is a supplement to, not a replacement for, professional mental health assistance and therapy.** If you feel deeply triggered by your shadow work or feel unequipped to face certain shadows on your own, please seek professional support.

## FULL MOON IN TAURUS

The full moon in Taurus is a reminder to seek out pleasure and ease even as you traverse the underworld of Scorpio season. While Scorpio is Persephone's descent into the underworld, Taurus is her return in the spring, bringing blossoming new life with her. You can think of the full moon in Taurus as a promise that Persephone and springtime will indeed return to the earth. This full moon is the perfect time for indulging in some sensual pleasures, getting a massage, and allowing life to feel easy.

What have I learned about embodying pleasure in the past six months?

_____

_____

_____

What does it mean for life to feel easy and pleasurable?

_____

_____

_____

How can I open my heart to even more pleasure in the future?

_____

_____

_____

## Sex Magick Body Oil

Scorpio season is the perfect opportunity to indulge in a little sex magick, which is excellent for healing, manifestation, and simple pleasure. That's because Scorpio is the sign of the Witch and of all things taboo: magick, death, darkness, even debt and inheritance (and, yes, sex). Scorpio is unashamed and unafraid of its potent, personal power and wants you to embrace your own personal power, too. Meanwhile, Taurus energy is all about pleasure and desire. Sex magick is a great way to get aligned with the energy of this Taurus-Scorpio axis.

Sex magick is really just the art of working with the intense energy that is raised during sex, whether alone or with a partner. It requires very little tools or experience, just a desire to embrace and love all parts of yourself and to pursue pleasure without shame. This sex magick body oil can be used solo or with a consenting partner (or partners) to tap into the magick of sexual pleasure and exploration.

- 2 parts dried rose petals (for intimacy)
- 1 part dried hibiscus (for passion and lust)
- 1 part dried damiana leaves (for sexual desire)
- 4–8 ounces pomegranate carrier oil (for desire and magick)

Fill a glass jar with the dried plant material. Pour the pomegranate oil over the dried plants so that they are completely covered. Store in a warm, dry place for at least one week, infusing under the light of the Taurus full moon if possible, and shaking the jar occasionally. When the oil is ready, strain the plant material out and pour the oil into a fresh jar, preferably fitted with a squeeze pump. Please note that this oil is intended to be applied externally as a massage oil or nourishing body oil, not an internal lubricant.

When ready to use, prepare your sacred space with care. Light black and white candles, place vases of red roses nearby or scatter rose petals, and cleanse your space by burning common sage, cedarwood, or even dried rosebuds. You might place smoky quartz (for Scorpio), and rose quartz (for Taurus) crystals your space as well. Set an intention for your sex magick experience, such as to manifest a desire into reality, to increase intimacy with your partner or with yourself, or simply to receive pleasure.

Undress and begin to anoint yourself and/or your partner with the body oil. Anoint your third eye, then your heartspace, then wherever feels good and right to you. Massage the oil into your shoulders, chest, and arms. Take the time to really discover the pleasure you can derive from this simple touch.

When you feel ready, move to pleasuring yourself and/or your partner. Build closer and closer to orgasm, edging away just as you almost reach the finish. Pull back at least two or three times, focusing on your intention and perhaps even stating it out loud over and over like an affirmation, until you fully reach orgasm, using the energy you've raised to also uplift and energize your intention.

# SAGITTARIUS SEASON (LATE NOVEMBER TO DECEMBER)

Sagittarius season is from approximately November 20 to December 19 each year, though it can shift a few days in either direction. Sagittarius is a carefree, adventurous, spiritual sign that's all about seeking wisdom in the most unexpected of places. During Sagittarius season, the darkest time of the year, you might tend to get a little restless. Sagittarius energy yearns to be out in nature, to connect with the wisdom of the wilderness, or even just to get out on the open road. This is a great time to allow yourself to feel in your bones what it truly means to be free.

- **Dates:** November 20–December 19
- **Season:** Autumn
- **Element:** Fire
- **Modality:** Mutable
- **Symbol:** The Archer
- **Archetype:** The Healer
- **Ruling Planet:** Jupiter (named for Roman god of the heavens)
- **Body Part:** Hips, thighs
- **Tarot Card:** Temperance, Queen of Wands

- **Color:** Orange
- **Goddesses:** Diana (Roman goddess of the hunt), Rhiannon (Welsh goddess of horses)
- **Plants:** Sage, dandelion, clove, hyssop
- **Crystals:** Pyrite, jasper

*Note: The above information is for the Northern Hemisphere. In the Southern Hemisphere, Sagittarius season, the new moon in Sagittarius, and the full moon in Gemini still occur in November and December but lead us through the transition from spring to summer, instead of from autumn to winter. Refer to the Gemini season section for correspondences, recipes, and rituals.*

# TRANSITION FROM AUTUMN TO WINTER

Sagittarius is the liminal space between the decaying leaves of autumn and the cold hibernation of winter. The darkest part of the year occurs during Sagittarius season. As the Healer of the zodiac, Sagittarius can find gifts and wisdom in any situation and has the power to help you heal yourself in the soothing cocoon of winter's rest. It's a beautiful time of year for learning, contemplating, and being in conversation with the wise ones (your spiritual leaders, the trees, your higher self, your closest friends, etc.).

How is the darkness supportive and necessary for healing?

_____

_____

_____

What gift does the darkest part of the year have for me?

_____

_____

_____

What final gratitude do I need to express before retreating within for the winter?

_____

_____

_____

## Essential Oils for Hiking

You might think of winter as a cold and desolate time of year when nature is decayed and in hibernation, but that period of hibernation is actually a beautiful gift! It's a reminder from the natural world that you are allowed, even encouraged, to rest. You might not think of going for a hike in late November or early December, but hiking can be a great way to connect with nature even as we head into the coldest season—just bundle up and be prepared for inclement weather.

Your Sagittarius season hike can be a walk along a nearby trail or a full-scale wilderness expedition, but the central goal is to connect with the wisdom and serenity of the natural world. These essential oils are great to bring along:

- **Lavender Essential Oil:** Apply to bruises and scrapes to soothe pain and heal damaged skin. Can also combat fall seasonal allergies (if you suffer year-round like I do!). Magickally, lavender is great for helping you open up to your intuition and higher self while communing with nature.

- **Peppermint Essential Oil:** Apply to wrists, collarbone, and behind your ears to repel bugs, inhale to clear sinuses, or rub into sore muscles to soothe. Magickally, peppermint is very helpful for banishing any negative thoughts or emotions and for allowing nature to cleanse your energy.
- **Tea Tree Essential Oil:** Apply to scrapes and bug bites to disinfect. Magickally, tea tree (or melaleuca) is very protective and purifying. Apply prior to your adventure to protect you on your journey.

Dilute all of these essential oils with a carrier oil such as sunflower, olive, or almond oil before applying directly to your skin. I recommend a ratio of no more than 5 to 8 drops of essential oil per 2 teaspoons of carrier oil.

## Apple Pear Galette

When the weather starts to turn cold and the holidays roll around, this cottage witch gets all kinds of inspired in the kitchen. Fall spices and fruits are perfect for satisfying my sudden baking kick, but I still like to keep things simple and accessible, so this apple pear galette is just the thing. Galettes are incredibly simple, rustic pies that you can make with pretty much whatever ingredients you have on hand. In this case, you're making use of pears for their sweet, delicious flavor and apples for their crisp texture and deeply magickal associations. Apples are actually one of the most magickal fruits, with a pentagram, the witch's symbol of the five elements (fire, earth, air, water, and spirit) found right in the center!

- 3 apples (for healing)
- 2 pears (for love)
- juice of 1 lemon (for purification)
- ⅓ cup dark brown sugar
- 1 tablespoon flour
- 1 tablespoon + 1 teaspoon cinnamon, divided (for power)
- 2 teaspoons ginger (for success)
- 1 teaspoon nutmeg (for luck)
- 1 prepackaged pastry crust (or the crust of your choosing)
- 2 tablespoons cold butter
- 2 tablespoons granulated sugar

Preheat the oven to 425°F. Line a baking sheet with parchment paper. Thinly slice the apples and pears and toss with the lemon juice, brown sugar, flour, 1 tablespoon cinnamon, ginger, and nutmeg. Lay the pastry crust out on the prepared baking sheet. Lay the apples and pears in concentric, overlapping circles starting in the center of the pastry crust and working your way out until there are about 2 to 3 inches of remaining crust around the outside edge. Fold the crust over the fruit in a rustic, casual way. Cut the butter into small cubes and place all over the top of the galette. Combine the granulated sugar with remaining cinnamon and sprinkle over the top. Bake for 45 to 50 minutes until golden brown. Remove to a cutting board to cool. Slice and enjoy!

## Orange-Clove Pomanders for Holiday Cheer

Sagittarius season is the transition from autumn into winter, leading us right up to the winter solstice. This season is full of such big, generous, celebratory energy because Sagittarius is one of the most vibrant and

generous signs in the zodiac, here to help us expand our mindset, experiences, and ability to love. These orange-clove pomanders are a favorite decoration in my house this time of year because they add a pop of color as we come into the darkest part of the year (and they smell wonderful, too!). I've always thought it was lovely that as the sun dips to its lowest point in the sky, citrus fruits come into season to bring us a bit of the sunshine and cheer that we might be missing.

- toothpick
- whole cloves (for protection and purification)
- medium orange (for happiness)
- 8"–10" ribbon

Use a toothpick to make pinpricks all over each of the oranges. You can make them random, in horizontal or vertical rows, or in zigzag or diamond patterns. Gently but firmly push the narrow tip of a whole clove into each pinprick. Place the orange in the center of your ribbon and tie the ribbon in a knot around the orange, then tie a bow in the remaining ends so that it can be used to hang the pomander. Hang your pomanders in windows, hallways, over mirrors, or anywhere you feel needs a boost of good energy and seasonal aromas.

## NEW MOON IN SAGITTARIUS

The new moon in Sagittarius is a time of freedom and wild abandon. Sagittarius is here to guide you to learn, grow, expand, go on adventures, and then embody and share everything you take in through the lens of your own inner wisdom. This new moon, consider setting intentions around expansion, healing, and trusting your own sense of knowing what is right and true for you.

What wisdom do I have naturally that I can share with others?

_____

_____

_____

How has my own healing journey helped me grow and expand?

_____

_____

_____

What can I do to embody my inner healer and share the wisdom I have with others?

_____

_____

_____

## Darkest Nights Tea for Turning Within

The new moon in Sagittarius is one of the darkest nights of the year, as it's both a night with no moonlight and one of the new moons closest to the winter solstice, the longest night of the year. This tea blend is designed to light up the darkest part of the year with spice and flavor, while still honoring that the darkness is a gift. This beautiful time of year is here to remind us to rest. We don't need to take action right now; we need to surrender to trust and faith in the season of turning within.

- 3 parts green tea (for inspiration)
- 2 parts roasted dandelion root (for wishes)
- 1 part meadowsweet (for peace)
- 1 part cardamom pods, gently crushed (for heart-centered reflection)
- star anise pods (for luck)

Combine all ingredients in a small bowl and stir to mix. Store in a glass jar in a cool, dry place. When ready to serve, scoop a tablespoon of the mixture into a tea infuser or empty tea bag and place in a mug. Pour hot water over the infuser or tea bag and allow to steep 1 to 3 minutes.

At the new moon in Sagittarius or in the days leading up to the winter solstice, enjoy a cup of this vibrant yet gentle tea. Light some white, yellow, or green candles to fill your space with warm, comforting light or sit and bask in the darkness. Pour a cup of tea and find a comfortable spot in your home or at your altar to sit and reflect. Tune into your heartspace, perhaps placing your hands over your heart, and close your eyes. Take a few deep breaths and imagine that there is a gentle green or golden glow emanating from your heart. Simply be here with this sensation, sipping your tea and basking in the glow of your heartspace. Allow any messages to come to you that desire to be heard and received. Reflect on how far you've come in the past year and how or why you might be ready for rest. Reflect on how rest can lead to expansion. You might journal or pull tarot cards on these questions or simply be present and mindful in this moment.

## FULL MOON IN GEMINI

The full moon in Gemini is a reminder not to take yourself too seriously. Where Sagittarius is the spiritual leader (and can sometimes border on a bit self-righteous), Gemini knows that there is no *one* answer to any question. Within every question, there are multitudes. This full moon is a perfect time for researching, taking a new course, engaging in conversation with other witches and spiritual people, and going all in on reflection journaling!

Where am I taking myself too seriously?

_____

_____

_____

How can I consider all sides and perspectives, while still trusting myself?

_____

_____

_____

What does it mean for there to be more than a single right answer to any question?

_____

_____

_____

## Yoga Mat Cleansing Spray

Yoga is a great tool for working with the Gemini-Sagittarius axis. Movements that encourage us to become more flexible in our minds and bodies are very aligned with Gemini's mutable, changeable energy and the spiritual, healing wisdom of the eight limbs of yoga goes straight to the heart of Sagittarius. This yoga mat cleansing spray is a favorite of mine because it's naturally purifying and smells great! All of the ingredients in this spray are both energetically and physically cleansing, so spritz this on your mat or into the air whenever you feel the need for a little psychic purification.

- ¾ cup dried common sage (for energetic cleansing)
- 4–6 ounces alcohol- and fragrance-free witch hazel (for purification)
- 12–15 drops cedarwood essential oil (for purification)
- 10–12 drops hyssop essential oil (for clearing away negativity)

Place the dried sage in a glass jar and pour the witch hazel over it until the sage is completely covered. Seal the jar and allow to infuse in a cool, dark place for 3 days. Strain the sage out of the infused witch hazel using a mesh strainer or a coffee filter. Pour the strained witch hazel, which should be fairly dark in color, into a clean glass jar fitted with a spray bottle cap and add the essential oils. Shake to combine. Charge under the light of the full moon if you so desire.

For your full moon ritual, light some yellow and orange candles, place Gemini crystals such as blue lace agate and chrysocolla around your mat, and have a journal nearby. Consider incorporating a yoga flow that honors the Gemini-Sagittarius axis. Gemini rules the shoulders, arms, hands, and lungs and Sagittarius rules the hips and thighs, so shoulder stretches, arm balances, and hip-opening poses are great options.

Afterward, grab a bolster or some pillows and blankets and get cozy on your mat with your journal. Gemini is the sign of words and communication and Sagittarius is all about our faith and spirituality, so this is a great time to do some journaling and visualizing what you want your practice to look like over the coming winter season. When you've completed your ritual, spritz your entire mat with the cleansing spray. Allow the mat to sit for a few minutes until it is no longer damp before rolling it up.

# Chapter 7
# WINTER

Winter is the season of hibernation, the most restful and reflective time of the year. This time of year is known for cold, dark nights gathered around the fireplace, delicious baked goods, and gathering with your loved ones. Energetically, winter is aligned with the element of earth. It's a relaxing day spent curled up by a snowy window with a warm blanket, a cup of tea, and a good book.

In terms of the seasonal, lunar, and astrological cycles, winter in the Northern Hemisphere is home to:

- Capricorn season, which begins at the winter solstice, and includes the Capricorn new moon and Cancer full moon.
- Aquarius season, which includes the festival of Imbolc, the Aquarius new moon, and Leo full moon.
- Pisces season, which leads us through the transition to spring and includes the Pisces new moon and Virgo full moon.

On the following pages, I'm going to share correspondences and recipes to help you embody and be in flow with all of these festivals, lunations, and seasonal rhythms!

Note: *In the Southern Hemisphere, Capricorn, Aquarius, and Pisces season occur during summer. If you live south of the equator, refer to the sections on the opposite signs, Cancer, Leo, and Virgo, for inspiration on celebrating these seasons.*

# CAPRICORN SEASON [LATE DECEMBER TO JANUARY]

Capricorn season is from approximately December 20 to January 19 each year, though it can shift a few days in either direction. Capricorn is a serious, structured, authoritative sign that's all about relying on and trusting the wisdom of your lived experiences. The deeper lesson of Capricorn is not to overcommit your resources by making choices and commitments that are sustainable.

- **Dates:** December 20–January 19
- **Season:** Winter
- **Element:** Earth
- **Modality:** Cardinal
- **Symbol:** The Sea Goat
- **Archetype:** The Crone
- **Ruling Planet:** Saturn (named for Roman god of time)
- **Body Part:** Skin, bones
- **Tarot Cards:** The Hierophant, The Devil
- **Color:** Charcoal gray
- **Goddesses:** Hekate (Greek crone goddess of witchcraft), Baba Yaga (Slavic folkloric witch)
- **Plants:** Rosemary, pine, cedar, cypress, mullein
- **Crystals:** Smoky quartz, aragonite

*Note: The above information is for the Northern Hemisphere. In the Southern Hemisphere, Capricorn season, the new moon in Capricorn, and the full moon in Cancer still occur in December and January but herald the beginning of the summer season instead of winter. Refer to the Cancer season section for correspondences, recipes, and rituals.*

# WINTER SOLSTICE

The winter solstice is the longest night of the year, the day with the least number of daylight hours. We celebrate this sabbat as our ancestors around the world have done for millennia: by bringing light to the darkness. Whether it's through stone monuments that align with the sun, candlelight, twinkle lights, or simply the bright, vibrant cheeriness of citrus fruit, humans have been lighting up the darkest day of the year far back into the depths of history.

How do I intend to rest and retreat during this darkest part of the year?

_____

_____

_____

Why must I create space for rest and hibernation before taking action again?

_____

_____

_____

What does it look like to bring light to the darkness of society?

_____

_____

_____

## Peppermint Chai for New Year Wishes

I started making this delicious peppermint chai one holiday season when I had an overabundance of mint and came up with the idea of a mint chai that would be replete with all the scents and flavors of the yuletide season. When I took my first sip of this delicious blend, I knew I had to share it. It's become one of my favorite cozy holiday beverages and gifts to give.

Capricorn season is both the longest night of the year and a day of brilliant hope, a reminder that every day after this until the summer solstice six months from now will be longer and longer as the sun slowly regains its power. Celebrate by lighting up the darkness with twinkle lights and candles and the bright, brilliant flavors of this peppermint chai.

- 3 parts dried peppermint leaves (for purification)
- 2 parts cinnamon sticks, gently crushed (for prosperity)
- 1 part whole cloves (for spiritual expansion)
- 1 part cardamom pods, gently crushed (for love)
- 1 part roasted dandelion root (for wishes)
- ½ part pink peppercorns (for following one's passions)

Combine all ingredients in a small bowl and stir to mix. Store in a glass jar in a cool, dry place. When ready to serve, scoop a tablespoon of the mixture into a tea infuser or empty tea bag. Place the infuser or tea bag in a mug and pour hot water over it. Allow to steep for at least 3 to 5 minutes.

Make a big pot of this tea for your friends and family or for yourself on the winter solstice or during Capricorn season. Set the pot in the center of the table or your altar and pass teacups to everyone. Light some white, green, or red candles and place mint or evergreen sprigs on the table. Place a small white chime candle in a paper or metal candle holder in front of everyone as well. As you pour the tea, ask everyone to share what they have loved most over the past year and what they've learned about themselves, life, and what it means to trust their own wisdom and experiences.

Once everyone has a cup of tea and has shared, ask each person to light their candle and to share what they want to learn and experience in the new year. As the sun begins to return, what do you wish to call into your life? Enjoy this time together, celebrating the sun's return.

## Evergreen Guardian Diffuser Blend

Most of the year, we are focused on flowering plants and deciduous trees with their brilliant fall colors. But in winter, our attention turns to the guardians of nature, whose ever-present green leaves and needles stand watch over the rest of the world while it slumbers through the winter. This lovely, cleansing diffuser blend is meant to connect you with the protective energy of the evergreen guardians to help you feel safe to rest and retreat during the winter season.

- 3 drops pine essential oil (for protection)
- 3 drops cedarwood essential oil (for protection)
- 2 drops fir essential oil (for protection)

Diffuse this blend in an ultrasonic or reed diffuser any time you need a boost of comfort and support.

Light white or green candles and place aragonite or smoky quartz crystals around you in a circle. Find a comfortable seated position and place your hands on your knees or wrap your arms around yourself in a comforting gesture. You might also place a blanket over your lap or shoulders, anything to make you feel cozy and comforted. Close your eyes and take a few deep, cleansing breaths. Begin to visualize a root growing out of the base of your spine and reaching down into the earth. It might grow around the rocks or meet other tree roots along the way as it tethers you to reality.

In your mind's eye, visualize a blank white space. Slowly, shapes and forms come into focus, and you are standing in a snow-covered forest. It is quiet and peaceful. There may be animals nearby; you may follow them. You can hear the crunch of snow underfoot but otherwise you are surrounded by the peaceful silence of snowfall. As you walk, you begin to see a cottage on the edge of the forest. It glows in the snow, warm and welcoming. You approach it and knock on the front door, taking notice of the door itself and what the cottage is built out of. The door swings open and you are welcomed inside.

Notice who welcomes you and who is present in this cozy space. You are given a cup of tea and a soft blanket to warm up by the fire. You feel a warm glow from inside of you as you sit with your welcoming hosts. When it comes times to leave, you thank them for their warm hospitality and bundle up again to head back out into the snow. You know that although this space is welcoming and cozy, the evergreen trees standing silent and tall in the snowy forest will also protect and guide you. Your hosts may give you something or share a message of wisdom for you to take with you. You step back outside into the snow and feel the crisp, cold air sting your cheeks. You walk back into the forest, back the way you came, into the silent, peaceful snowfall.

When you are ready, connect back with the roots anchoring you to the earth and to reality. Slowly return to your body, allowing the snowy forest to fade to white. Stretch your fingers and legs and open your eyes, carrying this supported feeling back into the rest of your day.

## Scented Pine Cones for Prosperity

Pine cones are one of those ubiquitous winter holiday decorations. Just like cedar garlands and wreaths, they come from the evergreen trees that are such a symbol of hope and life during the darkest days of winter. Pine trees are magickally associated with prosperity because they retain their evergreen needles throughout the winter months when most other plants lose their leaves and flowers and become barren. Practically speaking, pine cones seem to last forever and they're perfect for acting as both seasonal decoration and delicious smelling potpourri.

- pine cones (for prosperity)
- cookie sheet
- 1 gallon resealable bag
- 10 drops peppermint essential oil (for purification)
- 10 drops cinnamon essential oil (for protection)
- 10 drops orange essential oil (for prosperity)

Collect pine cones on a walk or from pine trees in your neighborhood. They could have dirt and bugs on them, since you are collecting them from nature, so be sure to wash them off thoroughly in the sink before using them for this project. Preheat the oven to 200°F. Place the pine cones on a baking sheet and bake for about an hour to dry them out and kill any remaining bugs or germs that might still be on them after rinsing.

Remove the pine cones from the oven and allow to cool completely, then transfer to your resealable plastic bag. Add the essential oils to the bag, being sure to drip on as many of the pine cones as possible, not just in one spot. Seal the bag, removing the air, and allow to sit for 1 to 2 weeks.

When you're ready, remove the pine cones to a bowl in your dining room or living room to scent the air with their delicious, cozy aroma.

This particular blend of essential oils not only smells wonderful but is also a great way to protect and purify your home in order to call in abundance and prosperity for the new year.

## NEW MOON IN CAPRICORN

Capricorn values structures and systems that help conserve energy and resources in practical, sustainable ways. Consider setting intentions at this new moon around career goals and creating structures to support your work, life, and self-care.

What do I want my work and public life to look like this month and moving into the new year?

_____

_____

_____

How can I channel my inner crone to strike a sustainable balance between working hard and resting when needed?

_____

_____

_____

What kinds of structures should I create as a foundation for my goals?

_____

_____

_____

## Rosemary Cranberry-Orange Cobbler for Legacy

The flavors and aromas of this cozy, holiday dessert are aligned with the classic energy of Capricorn, which values tradition and legacy, so this recipe is perfect for celebrating the new moon in Capricorn during the holiday season.

- 5 cups fresh cranberries (for courageous healing)
- ½ cup granulated sugar
- zest and juice of 1 orange (for joy)
- 2 tablespoons fresh rosemary, destemmed and finely chopped (for supportive foundations)
- 1 cup flour
- ½ cup brown sugar
- 1 teaspoon cinnamon (for spiritual protection)
- 1 teaspoon ginger (for love)
- ¼ cup milk
- 1 egg
- 4 tablespoons cold butter

Preheat oven to 350°F. Place the cranberries in a square baking dish and toss with the granulated sugar, orange zest and juice, and rosemary. In a small bowl, mix together the flour, brown sugar, and spices. Using a pastry blender or two knives, cut the butter into the dry mixture. Slowly add the milk and egg. Spoon the topping over the cranberry mixture. Bake for 45 to 50 minutes, or until golden brown. Remove from the oven and allow to cool slightly before serving.

This new moon is a great time for setting intentions around your own legacy and for establishing new traditions with your family. Gather together over this delicious snack to think about what you each want to do, have, experience, and be in the coming year, especially as it relates to work and to home and family. As you enjoy this delicious, soul-warming snack, contemplate your new year plans and how you can take courageous action toward strong foundations of healing.

## FULL MOON IN CANCER

The full moon in Cancer is a reminder to take time for deep rest, retreat, and reflection. While Capricorn is goal-oriented, Cancer is rest-oriented and values disconnecting from work and the need to achieve. This full moon is the perfect time for gazing up at the moon in all her brilliance (since this is the home sign of the moon), as well as taking time for a personal retreat to reflect and connect with your intuition.

How can I make more space for rest in my life?

_____

_____

_____

Where have I been pushing too hard and need to release some control?

_____

_____

_____

What do I need to take a break from?

_____

_____

_____

## Holiday Spiced Tub Tea

Tub teas are such a great way to bring the magick of herbs into your ritual bath. Cancer season always takes place around the holiday season, so this tub tea not only brings in herbs for intuitive, restful energy but also brings in the holiday scents that delight and inspire us.

- ½ cup eucalyptus leaves (for physical well-being)
- ½ cup cinnamon chips (for positive spiritual vibrations)
- ¼ cup pine needles or 5–8 drops pine essential oil (for purification)
- 5–8 drops myrrh essential oil (for deep contemplation)

Combine all ingredients in a bowl. Add the myrrh directly to the dried ingredients and stir to combine. Scoop the bath tea into a muslin bag and tie securely shut. When ready to use, place the muslin bag over the faucet of the tub so that the hot water runs through it into the bath. You can also submerge the bag directly in the hot water.

Arrange the bathroom for your ritual with white or green candles, crystals such as moonstone, and your favorite incense. Turn off any overhead lights for a soft, wintry glow; you might even string up some twinkle lights. Fill the tub using your holiday bath tea and rest your body in the soothing, warm water. Feel your entire body begin to relax and release any tension. You might even mentally scan your entire body starting at the crown of your head, down over your face, shoulders, and arms, over your torso and hips, and down your legs and feet, consciously relaxing each part of your body as you scan it.

You could do some divination or a meditation here or you might simply choose to relax and reflect. This full moon is an excellent time for some deeply nourishing self-care and reflection on how you want to honor your intuition in the coming year.

# AQUARIUS SEASON (LATE JANUARY TO FEBRUARY)

Aquarius season is from approximately January 20 to February 19 each year, though it can shift a few days in either direction. Aquarius is a rebellious, quirky sign that's all about social justice and honoring the individual within the collective. During Aquarius season, you might find yourself getting a little bit radical: setting radical boundaries around your self-care and mental health needs, standing up to fight against social injustices, and no longer sacrificing your well-being for unaligned people and projects.

- **Dates:** January 20–February 19
- **Season:** Winter
- **Element:** Air
- **Modality:** Fixed
- **Symbol:** The Water Bearer
- **Archetype:** The Rebel
- **Ruling Planet:** Uranus (named for Roman god of the sky)
- **Body Part:** Knees, shins
- **Tarot Card:** The Star, Justice
- **Color:** Light blue
- **Goddesses:** Aurora (Roman goddess of the dawn), Mayari (Tagalog goddess of revolution)

- **Plants:** Comfrey, witch hazel, cacao, air plants, bioluminescent mushrooms
- **Crystals:** Aura quartz, aquamarine

*Note: The above information is for the Northern Hemisphere. In the Southern Hemisphere, Aquarius season, the new moon in Aquarius, and the full moon in Leo still occur in January and February but sustain us through the summer season instead of winter. Refer to the Leo season section for correspondences, recipes, and rituals.*

# IMBOLC

Imbolc is the harbinger of spring, a promise that life is returning to the earth once more—and perhaps sooner than you might think. Imbolc is the last opportunity for rest, retreat, and radical self-care before you begin making plans and stepping into empowered, aligned action again at the spring equinox just a few short weeks away.

What do I need in order to feel deeply rested and nourished before spring comes?

_____

_____

_____

What does it mean for self-care or personal boundaries to be radical?

_____

_____

_____

How is the promise of springtime and of hopefulness manifesting in my own life?

_____

_____

_____

## Nourishing Milk Bath for Imbolc

Imbolc is perhaps one of the most overlooked of the eight pagan sabbats that form the Wheel of the Year, yet it's always been one of my own personal favorites. The main reason that Imbolc gets passed over is because it's one of the sabbats that, on the surface, least relates to modern, twenty-first century life. Some of the primary symbols of Imbolc are sheep and milk because this is the time of year when the ancient Celts were preparing for lambing season and milk was particularly abundant, but the more important and relevant overall theme of Imbolc is that this is the last rest of winter before the coming spring. This is an opportunity for deeply nourishing self-care and setting some boundaries with yourself and those around you in order to protect and nurture your most essential needs.

This milk bath is one of my favorite Imbolc rituals. It's perfect for nourishing dry, winter skin with the classic symbol of the season while reflecting on what your self-care needs truly are this year.

- 2 cups whole milk (for nourishing the body)
- ½ cup dried or fresh lavender flowers (for peace)
- 1 tablespoon whole cloves (for positive spiritual vibrations)
- 4–6 drops lavender essential oil (for peace)
- 2 tablespoons reishi mushroom powder (for nourishing the spirit)

Warm the milk on the stove or in the microwave so it is warm to the touch but not scalding. Pour the milk into a bowl or dish large enough to submerge both of your hands or feet. Add the other ingredients and gently stir to combine until the mushroom powder is dissolved. If you prefer a full-body milk bath, double the recipe and add to a hot bath.

Light some white candles and set yourself up with a cozy space, including soft blankets and pillows, relaxing music, and dim lights or candlelight. Pour yourself a cup of tea and take a moment to unwind. Roll your shoulders a few times, close your eyes, and focus on your breath. Allow yourself to become fully and wholly present. Sink your hands or feet (or your whole body if choosing to do a full-body milk bath) into the warm milk mixture. Allow peace and calm to settle over you, nourishing both your body and your spirit.

This is a great opportunity to do some meditation and to visualize the nourishment of the milk, mushrooms, spices, and flowers soaking into your body and replenishing your energy and vitality.

## Spiked & Spiced Hot Cocoa

My go-to coffee shop order is a spicy almond chai latte, but some wintry days the only thing that will satisfy is a deliciously rich cup of hot cocoa. Something about hot chocolate topped off with whipped cream just takes you right back to childhood, doesn't it? And there's something playful about Aquarius season that delights in the delights of our youth. This spicy take on the classic cocoa recipe with an adults-only upgrade option makes this Imbolc season concoction both spiced *and* spiked!

- 8 ounces milk of your choice (for nurturing)
- 2 tablespoons raw cacao powder (for grounded support from the ancestors)

- 2 teaspoons ground cinnamon (for healing hearts)
- pinch ground cayenne (for spiritual strength)
- 1–2 ounces brandy (optional)
- dollop homemade vanilla whipped cream (optional)

Place the milk in a small saucepan on the stove and scoop in the cacao and spices. Stir continuously until the powders have dissolved and the milk is completely warmed through to your desired temperature. Pour into a large mug and top with brandy, stirring to combine, and homemade vanilla whipped cream. (To make the whipped cream, simply whip a half pint of heavy whipping cream, a teaspoon of vanilla, and a tablespoon of sugar in a mixer on high speed until it is light and creamy.) Enjoy this delicious treat in front of a cozy fireplace or an altar adorned with white candles.

## Candle Dressing Oil for Prioritizing Self-Care

Candles are another essential element of Imbolc. (In fact, the Christianized name for Imbolc is "Candlemas.") There is something so cozy and comforting about the glow of a candle flame from a white candle, reflected in windows and mirrors on a cold winter evening. Imbolc season is one of my favorite times of the year for practicing self-care rituals and for taking the time to reflect on what my self-care needs truly are.

This candle dressing oil is designed to serve as an opportunity to reflect on and reevaluate your self-care rituals as a whole. Use it at Imbolc or whenever your self-care practices need a bit of a refresh!

- 2 teaspoons carrier oil such as sunflower or olive oil
- 2–3 drops angelica essential oil (for renewal)

- 2–3 drops fir essential oil (for clearing the mind)
- 1–2 drops lavender essential oil (for consecrating the sacred self)

Combine the oils in a small bowl, mixing them gently. Alternatively, you could combine them in a bottle fitted with a roller ball cap. Take a white birthday or chime candle and hold it in one hand. Dip your fingers in the oil mixture and rub the oil onto the candle, starting from the bottom and working your way up to the middle, then from the top down to the middle. If using a roller ball bottle, simply roll the oil onto the candle from bottom to middle and top to middle. Rubbing the oil into the center of the candle is to call in energy, as opposed to banishing it.

Place the candle in a fire-safe holder on your altar and strike a match. As you light the candle, say out loud or silently to yourself, "I nourish my spiritual, physical, mental, and emotional needs." You may want to light several candles on your altar, anointing some or all of them with the oil, as is customary at Imbolc.

As the candles burn, open your journal or grimoire to a new, blank page. At the top, write "The Pillars of My Spiritual Self-Care Practice." Create headings for Mind, Body, Intuition, Nature, and Devotion, leaving yourself space to journal under each. Reflect on what level you currently feel fulfilled in each of these areas and brainstorm practices that you might be able to change or introduce into your self-care rituals to fulfill yourself more completely in each. You might also choose to do some fire scrying (gazing into the candle flame to receive messages or visions) or pull tarot or oracle cards to help you with your reflections.

# NEW MOON IN AQUARIUS

The new moon in Aquarius is a time of rebellion and change, when you may find yourself wanting to rebel against society, boundaries, and even what you thought you wanted. Aquarius is all about seeking progress and change for the good of the collective. This new moon, consider setting intentions for pursuing social justice and pushing your own boundaries.

What actions can I take in the next month to actively pursue social justice?

_____

_____

_____

Where do I have boundaries in my self-care, beliefs, and relationships and are they currently serving me?

_____

_____

_____

How does my inner rebel want me to revolutionize my life or perspective?

_____

_____

_____

## Constellation Clay Diffuser Necklace

New moons are the ideal time for stargazing throughout the year because the sky is especially dark with no moonlight. Since Aquarius is the sign that rules astrology and astronomy, the new moon in Aquarius is particularly energetically aligned. Some years, the new moon in Aquarius even coincides with the Alpha Centauroids, a minor meteor shower.

Clay diffuser jewelry is a really fun project and a great way to take the magick and healing power of essential oils with you wherever you go. In this case, you'll be stamping the necklaces with the astrology sign or constellation of your choice, so you'll be taking the energy of that sign and archetype with you as well.

- air-dry clay
- toothpick or chopstick
- cord or chain
- 1–3 drops essential oil of choice

Separate the air-dry clay into small balls, about 1–1½ inches in diameter, for as many necklaces as you would like to make. Gently flatten the balls so that they form flattened circles, about ¼–⅜ inch thick. Use a toothpick or chopstick to gently punch a hole in the top of the circle, about ¼ inch from the edge, for the cord or chain to be strung through. Then, use your toothpick or chopstick to either draw the astrology sign symbol of your choosing in the clay or to make an impression of each star in the sign's constellation. If you choose to make a constellation, press about halfway into the clay but do not punch a hole all the way through.

Allow your clay to dry for 1 to 3 days. Alternatively, you can use oven-baked clay, which is dried in the oven. When your clay necklace is dry, string the cord or chain through it and place 1 to 3 drops of your favorite essential oil on the clay to diffuse it throughout your day.

For your new moon in Aquarius stargazing ritual, you might choose an essential oil that's associated with the new moon, such as lavender or peppermint, or an essential oil that's associated with Aquarius, such as rosemary. As you look up at the stars, allow your eyes to adjust to the darkness so you can really see the brilliant, twinkling lights above and reflect on the vastness of the cosmos. Find peace and serenity in knowing that you are part of a great collective of humanity and cosmic life.

# FULL MOON IN LEO

The full moon in Leo is a reminder to have some fun and stay playful even when the world seems to be against you. While Aquarius is immersed in the quest for equality and justice through political action and allyship, Leo knows that sometimes the most impactful act of rebellion is just being yourself unapologetically. This full moon is the perfect time to do some art magick and say self-love affirmations in the mirror.

How does me loving myself help smash the patriarchy?

_____

_____

_____

What does it mean for me to be unapologetically myself?

_____

_____

_____

How can my art (whatever form I express myself in) support the collective?

_____

_____

_____

## Creativity Boosting London Fog Latte

When I'm not sipping a cup of herbal tea or a chai latte, a delicious London Fog is my next go-to. The classic London Fog steps your Earl Grey tea up a notch with frothed and sweetened hot milk and this recipe takes it even further by adding additional herbs and flowers. The full moon in Leo is a time of abundant celebration, unapologetic self-love, and bold self-expression. This tea latte will give your creativity a boost and help you find the confidence to express yourself during this magickal and expressive time.

- 1 tablespoon Earl Grey tea leaves (for a boost of success)
- 1 teaspoon dried chamomile flowers (for stimulating creativity)
- 1 teaspoon dried orange peel (for self-confidence)
- ¾ cup hot water
- ¾ cup milk of your choice
- ¼ teaspoon vanilla extract
- 1 teaspoon raw honey or 1 tablespoon brown sugar

Combine the Earl Grey tea, chamomile flowers, and orange peel in a tea infuser or empty tea bag and place in a mug. Pour ¾ cup hot water over the infuser and allow to steep 3 to 5 minutes. Bring milk to a boil on the stovetop. Stir the vanilla into the milk gently with a wooden spoon. Pour the warmed milk into a French press to froth (you can skip this step if you do not have a French press available). Remove the tea infuser and dissolve the honey or brown sugar in the hot tea. Top with the milk, frothed or simply hot. Garnish with chamomile flowers, if desired. Stir gently and serve warm.

As you enjoy this delicious beverage, break out your favorite craft project, a coloring book, or an art or writing project you haven't looked at in a while. Visualize a warm, glowing orange or yellow light infusing your being with every sip, filling you up with the creativity and joy of the sun itself, the ruler of this full moon in Leo.

## PISCES SEASON (LATE FEBRUARY TO MARCH)

Pisces season is from approximately February 20 to March 19 each year, though it can shift a few days in either direction. Pisces is a highly intuitive and empathic sign that's all about transcending the bounds of reality and of the tangible world. During Pisces season, you're reaching the release point of the annual cycle. You may find yourself reflecting on the past year, discovering what lessons you learned and what growth was made, and then releasing and letting go of what no longer serves you. This is the time of year when you get to decide what you are bringing with you into the next cycle—and what you're leaving behind.

- **Dates:** February 20–March 19
- **Season:** Winter
- **Element:** Water
- **Modality:** Mutable
- **Symbol:** The Fish
- **Archetype:** The Oracle
- **Ruling Planet:** Neptune (named for Roman god of the sea)

- **Body Part:** Feet
- **Tarot Card:** The Moon, Queen of Cups
- **Color:** Purple
- **Goddesses:** Sirona (Celtic goddess of healing springs), Yemaya (Yoruba goddess of the ocean)
- Plants: Mugwort, kelp, bladderwrack, valerian, blueberry
- Crystals: Fluorite, amethyst

Note: *The above information is for the Northern Hemisphere. In the Southern Hemisphere, Pisces season, the new moon in Pisces, and the full moon in Virgo still occur in February and March but lead us through the transition from summer to autumn, instead of from winter to spring. Refer to the Virgo season section for correspondences, recipes, and rituals.*

## TRANSITION FROM WINTER TO SPRING

Although I've referred to all of the mutable seasons as liminal spaces, this feels most authentic for Pisces season, the transition from the cold depths of winter to the hopefulness of springtime. Pisces is perhaps the most mutable and changeable of the signs. In fact, it's said that as the final sign in the zodiac, Pisces contains all the wisdom and healing (and wounds), of all the signs that came before it. Pisces is karma and endings and beginnings and renewal.

What does it mean for Pisces to contain all the wisdom and wounds of all the signs in the zodiac?

_____

_____

_____

What am I releasing from the past year before moving into a new one?

_____

_____

_____


How have I evolved and become a new person since this time last year?

_____

_____

_____

## Infused Sea Salt for Empathic Protection

Infusing salts and sugars is one of my favorite ways to dress up items we use pretty much daily in the kitchen. This is a great form of easy, natural kitchen magick! Pisces is perhaps the "wateriest" of the three water signs, as it is a mutable sign, embodying the changeable, flowing nature of water. Sea salt is a great way to connect with Pisces energy since it comes from the very oceans themselves.

Infused sea salts are often used as "finishing salts," a garnish on top of a finished dish or even on a slice of buttered bread (so delicious!). Magickally, salt is often used for purification and protection, so it's an excellent ingredient for shielding your energy, especially when combined with other delicious and protective ingredients. This recipe is particularly useful for those with empathic gifts, who often feel very open and sensitive to the emotions of others.

- ½ cup unrefined sea salt (for purification and protection)
- 2 tablespoons lemon zest (for purification)

- 1 tablespoon dried basil (for psychic protection)
- 1 tablespoon dried elderflower (for protection, especially while dreaming)

Place all ingredients in a food processor and pulse until evenly combined or grind in a mortar and pestle. Store in a glass jar in a cool, dry place.

Find a comfortable, safe, and quiet space to sit on the floor. Fill the bottom of a small dish with your protective, infused sea salt and place a white candle in the center of the dish. Set it on the floor in front of you. Sprinkle a bit of sea salt or even just table salt in a circle all the way around you, enclosing you, the dish, and the candle. You might also place some clear quartz crystals around you as well.

Light the candle and close your eyes. Visualize a purifying and protective light pouring out from the candle and coming up around your entire being, enclosing you in a protective bubble. Feel the light and salt purifying you of the energy, negativity, or emotions of others so that you can truly feel your own self. Imagine that the light is soaking into your body (your physical body and also your energetic body), forming a protective layer of energy that glows along your skin.

Stay here in peaceful meditation as long as you feel called to. When you feel complete, extinguish the candle, then break the circle of salt to close your sacred space. You can also sprinkle this delicious, infused sea salt on top of your favorite dishes to consume its protective energy. Monthly or weekly protection rituals are really supportive for those with strong intuitive and empathic gifts.

## Self-Care Foot Soak

The term "self-care" began as a radical revolt against the inequities of the Western health-care system, especially by women of color and LGBTQIA2 folx. But at some point, "self-care" became co-opted by mass media and capitalism and was turned into an expensive and indulgent treat like pedicures, bubble baths, and skipping work.

I believe that true self-care exists somewhere on that very wide spectrum and that indulgence is sometimes needed but soul-level nurturing is needed more. Now, that doesn't mean you have to swear off pedicures or bubble baths, but it's important to make use of them in meaningful and impactful ways. A pedicure isn't a replacement for other types of self-care; it's just one element in a holistic practice.

Pisces rules the feet, so taking extra care of your feet with a soothing pedicure or foot soak during Pisces season is a great way to align yourself with the energy of this sign. And you don't need to leave behind the deeper, more metaphoric level of self-care to be found here, either. Nurturing your feet is about nurturing your foundations and taking "steps" toward balance in self-care.

- 8–12 cups warm water
- 1 cup Epsom salts
- ½ cup fresh or dried lavender flowers (for peace and purification)
- ¼ cup fresh or dried mugwort leaves (for healing)
- 3–5 drops eucalyptus essential oil (for balance)

Pour the warm water into a small bucket or foot bath and add the salts, herbs, and oil. You may need to allow the water to cool slightly, so test it before submerging your bare feet.

Set yourself up with a comfortable chair, cozy blanket, some candles and crystals, and a good book or even a movie to watch as you soak your feet. But first, before turning your attention to total relaxation and escapism, grab your journal and reflect on the following prompts:

How do my spiritual or intuitive wellness and my physical wellness intersect or overlap?

_____

_____

_____

Am I nurturing all aspects of myself (spiritual, physical, mental, and emotional)?

_____

_____

_____

How am I currently caring for my foundations and most essential needs?

_____

_____

_____

## Smoke Cleansing Bundle for Releasing

We all have things we need to release, and although the waning moon every month is a beautiful time for ongoing release work, sometimes you need to go deeper. Pisces season provides that opportunity. Release work is about releasing the shadows, blocks, and limiting beliefs that are holding you back; releasing fear, shame, anger, or guilt; and releasing the situations, things, and people who are no longer serving your highest good. This smoke cleansing bundle is designed to support you in your releasing rituals so that you can move into the new astrological year with a fresh, clean slate–but feel free to also use it during waning moon rituals or anytime during the year when you need to release and let go!

- 3–5 stems fresh yarrow (for banishing)
- 3–5 stems fresh lavender (for releasing negativity)
- 5–10 fresh rose petals (for healing the heart)
- 1–3 small cypress branches (for healing grief and fear)
- scissors
- 3 pieces twine

Lay all the herbs on the table together. With your scissors, trim to the same length, about six inches. Lay all the pieces of twine on the table about an inch and a half apart and place the herbs on top. Layer the rose petals over the herbs. Tie the twine around the herbs and over the petals securely, then knot and trim off the ends. Hang your bundle to dry for a few days up to a week or two.

For your releasing ritual, find a comfortable spot at your altar, somewhere in your home, or outside. Place a fire-safe bowl or shell on the table in front of you. You might also want to set up some white or blue candles and fluorite or amethyst crystals nearby. Using a match or lighter, light the end of the smoke cleansing bundle so that smoke begins to emerge from it. If it physically lights with flame, just gently blow it out. Hold the bundle in front of you and speak out loud or to yourself, "I release my fears, shadows, and limiting beliefs and surrender them to the universe." Wave the smoke gently around you, perhaps walking into different corners of the room in a counterclockwise motion and repeating the affirmation.

Return to your seat and hold the bundle in front of you again. Name out loud for yourself, or silently in your head, the specific things, situations, activities, or beliefs that you are choosing to release. Wave the smoke gently around your body, breathing in deeply. Wave the smoke into the corners of the room and around your body. Place the bundle in the fire-safe bowl and take this opportunity to journal about the space you are creating in your life by releasing these unaligned experiences or pull tarot cards or use another divination tool. Relight the bundle as necessary and when you are finished, extinguish it safely. Do not leave the bundle burning if you need to leave the room.

## NEW MOON IN PISCES

The new moon in Pisces is a time of contradictions—it's the release point in the year, the last new moon before the spring equinox, yet it's considered the moon phase for new beginnings and setting intentions. I like to use this new moon as an opportunity to connect with my intuition and reflect on the intentions I will be setting for the year at the new moon in Aries the following month.

How can I connect with my intuition more intentionally this month?

_____

_____

_____

What goals for the next year is my inner oracle guiding me to set?

_____

_____

_____

What do I need to release before the astrological new year?

_____

_____

_____

## Mugwort Dream Tea

Dreaming is perhaps one of Pisces's most important superpowers. Although working with divination tools and ritual baths are excellent options for connecting with your intuition during Pisces season and throughout the year, I really believe that your dreams are the most potent divination "tool" you have at your disposal. That's because your dreams are an uninhibited direct line to your intuition and higher self, not filtered through the symbolism and assigned meaning of a tool like tarot. Similarly, and relatedly, mugwort is one of the most powerful herbs in a witch's day-to-day arsenal. It helps you connect with your intuition, open up to your spirit guides, and receive wisdom via your dreams.

This mugwort and valerian dream tea is ideal for aiding you in this process of opening up, surrendering, and receiving. It is very likely to make you quite sleepy so you should only drink this tea before going to bed, not before you need to do anything or drive anywhere.

- 3 parts white peony tea leaves (for calm)

- 2 parts dried lavender flowers or chamomile flowers (for peaceful dreams)
- 1 part dried mugwort leaves (for intuitive wisdom)
- 1 part dried valerian leaves (for deep sleep)
- ½ part dried marshmallow root (for grounding)

Combine all ingredients in a small bowl and stir to mix. Store in a glass jar in a cool, dry place. When ready to serve, scoop a tablespoon of the mixture into a tea infuser or empty tea bag. Place the infuser or tea bag in a mug and pour hot water over it. Allow to steep for 2 to 3 minutes.

Set up a dream altar on your nightstand, including some crystals for peace and intuition, such as amethyst and selenite, perhaps a reed diffuser for some relaxing essential oils like lavender, and a journal and pen. Get into your pajamas, set your pillows up just right, and make sure you have plenty of blankets. We're striving for comfort here so that you can relax into a deep sleep and access your dreams with ease. Turn off all your devices and any electronic lights in the room, as these can be very disruptive to REM sleep. Sip your tea slowly and reflectively, allowing your body to completely relax. Intentionally relax your shoulders, jaw, and even your tongue in your mouth. Do some deep breathing or listen to some soft relaxing music or a guided meditation.

Allow yourself to drift peacefully off to sleep. When you wake, immediately reach for your journal and write down anything you can recall about your dreams. This might just be flashes of memory, colors, or images, and it might not make a lot of sense in the moment, but get it all on paper before it leaves your consciousness. Later, after you've fully awoken or even the following night, come back to your dream journal and review what you've written. Reflect and journal on any themes or symbols that seem to emerge or stand out for you.

# FULL MOON IN VIRGO

The full moon in Virgo is a reminder to ground your intuition in reality. While Pisces is an open channel for messages of all kinds, Virgo is here to gently remind you to be a bit more practical. This full moon is perfect for rituals that guide you to access your intuition for answers to specific questions or to get grounded in your intuition.

What practical questions am I truly craving answers to?

_____

_____

_____

What does it mean to access my intuition in a practical way?

_____

_____

_____

How can I ground my intuitive hits in reality?

_____

_____

_____

## Dream Priestess Pillow & Sheet Spray

There is such a beautiful magick and balance in the Virgo-Pisces axis because it truly encompasses every facet of humanity, from our day-to-day lives and tasks to the transcendent, mystical experiences we can't quite describe in words. The Virgo-Pisces axis is the rainbow bridge between the tangible or "mundane" world and the spiritual, mystical realm.

The archetypes of these two signs beautifully state their interdependence. Virgo is the Priestess, facilitating spiritual connection between the earth and the heavens so that Pisces, the Oracle, can receive messages and wisdom from the divine. Without the grounded facilitation of the Priestess, the Oracle would not have a context in which to deliver their wisdom.

The final recipe in this book is designed to combine these two archetypes of the zodiac to create a ritual that helps you become a Dream Priestess, Priest, or Priestexx of your very own, to facilitate connection in the physical plane so that your spirit can fly in the dream realm.

- 10–15 drops lavender essential oil (for peaceful dreams)
- 10–15 drops rosemary essential oil (for remembering dreams upon waking)
- 8–10 drops vetiver essential oil (for balancing the spiritual and mundane)
- 5–8 drops valerian essential oil (for deep sleep)
- 1 ounce alcohol- and fragrance-free witch hazel (for purification)
- 2.5–3 ounces distilled water

Using a dropper, place the essential oils into a 4-ounce amber or cobalt glass jar and top with the witch hazel. Add distilled water to fill the container and fit with a spray bottle lid. Shake the bottle to combine, then allow to sit for preferably at least a day or two in a cool place away from sunlight.

Before bed on the full moon in Virgo or anytime that you intend to practice dream work, spritz your pillowcases and sheets with this Dream Priestess spray to encourage psychic dreams and intuitive visions that you can remember and apply in your waking life. You might even pair this with the Mugwort Dream Tea (page 239)!

# Appendix
## Recipes by Season

## SPRING

# SUMMER

# AUTUMN

# WINTER

# Recipes by Moon Sign (New and Full Moon)

New Moon in Aries: Candle Dressing Blend for Inspiration, page 96

Full Moon in Aries: Spiced Apple Chai for the Harvest Moon, page 176

New Moon in Taurus: Inner Goddess Rosebud Tea, page 109

Full Moon in Taurus: Sex Magick Body Oil, page 192

New Moon in Gemini: The Magician Tea + Tarot Spread, page 121

Full Moon in Gemini: Yoga Mat Cleansing Spray, page 203

New Moon in Cancer: Ocean Tides Healing Bath Salts, page 135

Full Moon in Cancer: Holiday Spiced Tub Tea, page 218

New Moon in Leo: Hair Oil for Nourishing Your Lion's Mane, page 147

Full Moon in Leo: Creativity Boosting London Fog Latte, page 229

New Moon in Virgo: Priestess Candle Dressing Oil, page 158

Full Moon in Virgo: Dream Priestess Pillow & Sheet Spray, page 242

New Moon in Libra: Bath Salts for Inner & Outer Balance, page 174

Full Moon in Libra: Balanced Self Crystal Elixir, page 99

New Moon in Scorpio: Shadow Work Tea, page 188

Full Moon in Scorpio: Love Spell Anointing Oil, page 111

New Moon in Sagittarius: Darkest Nights Tea for Turning Within, page 201

Full Moon in Sagittarius: Smoke Cleansing Bundle for Intuitive Wisdom, page 123

New Moon in Capricorn: Rosemary Cranberry-Orange Cobbler for Legacy, page 216

Full Moon in Capricorn: Full Moon Anointing Oil for Grounding, page 138

New Moon in Aquarius: Constellation Clay Diffuser Necklace, page 226

Full Moon in Aquarius: Luminary Tea Blend for Community Support, page 149

New Moon in Pisces: Mugwort Dream Tea, page 239

Full Moon in Pisces: Bath Tea for Nourishing Intuition, page 161

# Recipes by Type

## DIFFUSER BLENDS

## ANOINTING OILS

## CANDLE DRESSING OILS

## BATH & BODY PRODUCTS

## CLEANSING

## TEAS

## DESSERTS

## DRINKS

## SAVORY RECIPES

## PROJECTS & CRAFTS

# Recipes by Plant

ANGELICA: *Peace, renewal*

Botanical Gin, page 168

Candle Dressing Oil for Prioritizing Self-Care, page 224

Ocean Tides Healing Bath Salts, page 135

APPLE: *Magick, manifestation, healing*

Apple Pear Galette, page 197

Festive Harvest Cocktail, page 170

Spiced Apple Chai for the Harvest Moon, page 176

BASIL: *Fertility, desire, psychic protection*

Infused Sea Salt for Empathic Protection, page 232

Priestess Candle Dressing Oil (for Lakshmi), page 158

BLACKBERRY: *Wealth, healing, reflection*

Iced Blackberry Lime Mint Tea, page 152

Late Summer Harvest Sangria, page 143

BLADDERWRACK: *Psychic ability*

Bath Tea for Nourishing Intuition, page 161

CACAO/CHOCOLATE: *Self-love, grounding, ancestral connection*

Pomegranate Chocolate Bites, page 180

Spiked & Spiced Hot Cocoa, page 222

## CINNAMON: *Success, passion, protection, power, prosperity, positive spiritual vibrations, healing*

Apple Pear Galette, page 197

Botanical Gin, page 168

Gratitude Diffuser Blend, page 170

Holiday Spiced Tub Tea, page 218

Peppermint Chai for New Year Wishes, page 210

Roasted Sweet & Spicy Pumpkin Seeds, page 187

Rosemary Cranberry-Orange Cobbler for Legacy, page 216

Scented Pine Cones for Prosperity, page 213

Spiced Apple Chai for the Harvest Moon, page 176

Spiked & Spiced Hot Cocoa, page 222

Waxing Moon Charm Bag for Taking Action, page 49

## CLOVE: *Protection, purification, expansion, positive spiritual vibrations*

Botanical Gin, page 168

Nourishing Milk Bath for Imbolc, page 221

Orange-Clove Pomanders for Holiday Cheer, page 198

Peppermint Chai for New Year Wishes, page 210

Priestess Candle Dressing Oil, page 158

## CORIANDER

Botanical Gin, page 168

## CRANBERRY: *Courage, healing*

Rosemary Cranberry-Orange Cobbler for Legacy, page 126

Evergreen Guardian Diffuser Blend, page 211

Priestess Candle Dressing Oil (for Inanna), page 158

## FRANKINCENSE: *Positive spiritual vibrations, protection*

Priestess Candle Dressing Oil, page 158

Rosewater Facial Toner for Self-Love, page 102

## GERANIUM: *Fertility, love*

Hair Oil for Nourishing Your Lion's Mane, page 147

Love Spell Anointing Oil, page 111

## GINGER: *Success, love*

Apple Pear Galette, page 197

Rosemary Cranberry-Orange Cobbler for Legacy, page 216

## GOLDENSEAL: *Manifestation*

Waxing Moon Charm Bag for Taking Action, page 49

## GRAPEFRUIT: *Purification, inspiration*

Bath Tea for Nourishing Intuition, page 161

Candle Dressing Oil for Inspiration, page 96

New Moon Diffuser Blend for Clarity, page 45

Spring Cleansing Spray, page 93

## HIBISCUS: *Love, lust, passion*

Inner Goddess Rosebud Tea, page 109

Sex Magick Body Oil, page 192

## LEMON: *Cleansing, fresh starts, love, friendship, purification*

## LEMONGRASS: *Mental and intuitive clarity*

## LEMON VERBENA: *Positive habits, purification*

Astrological New Year Intention Setting Tea, page 92

The Magician Tea, page 121

## LIME: *Healing, inspiration*

Iced Blackberry Lime Mint Tea, page 152

Ocean Tides Healing Bath Salts, page 135

## MARSHMALLOW: *Gentleness, grounding*

Inner Goddess Rosebud Tea, page 109

Mugwort Dream Tea, page 239

## MEADOWSWEET: *Holding space, peace*

Darkest Nights Tea for Turning Within, page 201

Luminary Tea Blend for Community Support, page 149

## MUGWORT: *Astral Travel, visualization, healing, intuitive wisdom, dreams*

Mugwort Dream Tea, page 239

Self-Care Foot Soak, page 235

The Magician Tea, page 121

## MYRRH: *Deep contemplation, meditation*

Holiday Spiced Tub Tea, page 218

## NECTARINE: *Hope, abundance*

Late Summer Harvest Sangria, page 143

Moonwater Sun Tea, page 130

## NEROLI: *Communicating with the spirit realm*

Bath Tea for Nourishing Intuition, page 161

## NUTMEG: *Abundance, success, determination, luck*

Apple Pear Galette, page 197

Gratitude Diffuser Blend, page 170

Shadow Work Tea, page 188

Spiced Apple Chai for the Harvest Moon, page 176

## OATS/WHEAT: *Abundance, prosperity*

Luminary Tea Blend for Community Support, page 149

Wheat Wreath for Abundance, page 144

## ORANGE: *Self-Awareness, happiness, prosperity, joy, self-confidence*

Botanical Gin, page 168

Creativity Boosting London Fog Latte, page 229

Orange-Clove Pomanders for Holiday Cheer, page 198

Rosemary Cranberry-Orange Cobbler for Legacy, page 216

Scented Pine Cones for Prosperity, page 213

Shadow Work Tea, page 188

Waxing Moon Charm Bag for Taking Action, page 49

## PATCHOULI: *Consecration, communicating with spirits*

Candle Dressing Oil for Ancestor Veneration, page 182

Sacred Space Diffuser Blend for Daily Rituals, page 154

## PEAR: *Love*
Apple Pear Galette, page 197

## PEPPERCORNS (BLACK): *Action, protection*
Botanical Gin, page 168

Priestess Candle Dressing Oil (for Athena/Minerva), page 158

Spiced Apple Chai for the Harvest Moon, page 176

## PEPPERCORNS (PINK): *Love, following your passion*
Peppermint Chai for New Year Wishes, page 210

Spiced Apple Chai for the Harvest Moon, page 176

## PEPPERMINT: *Communication, clarity, change, inspiration, purification, banishing, releasing*
Communication Clarity Diffuser Blend, page 117

Essential Oils for Hiking, page 196

Iced Blackberry Lime Mint Tea, page 152

Lavender Mint Whipped Body & Hand Butter, page 118

Peppermint Chai for New Year Wishes, page 210

Scented Pine Cones for Prosperity, page 213

Shadow Work Tea, page 188

The Magician Tea Blend, page 121

Watermelon Sorbet for Emotional Cleansing, page 132

## PINE: *Grounding, protection, prosperity, purification*
Evergreen Guardian Diffuser Blend, page 211

Full Moon Anointing Oil for Grounding, page 138

Holiday Spiced Tub Tea, page 218

Scented Pine Cones for Prosperity, page 213

## POMEGRANATE: *Loving your shadows, connecting with the underworld, magick, desire*

Love Spell Anointing Oil, page 111

Pomegranate Chocolate Bites, page 180

Priestess Candle Dressing Oil (for Persephone/Proserpina), page 158

Sex Magick Body Oil, page 192

## PUMPKIN: *Abundance*

Jack-O'-Lantern Carving, page 185

Roasted Sweet & Spicy Pumpkin Seeds, page 187

## REISHI MUSHROOM: *Nourishing the Spirit*

Nourishing Milk Bath for Imbolc, page 221

## ROSE: *Self-love, love, opening the heart, healing the heart, psychic ability, intimacy*

Full Moon Tea for Reflection, page 52

Inner Goddess Rosebud Tea, page 109

Love Spell Anointing Oil, page 111

Priestess Candle Dressing Oil (for Aphrodite/Venus or Freya), page 158

Rosewater Facial Toner for Self-Love, page 102

Sex Magick Body Oil, page 192

Smoke Cleansing Bundle for Releasing, page 236

ROSEMARY: *Focus, purification, clarity, healing, remembering the dead, supportive foundations, memory*

SAGE: *Purification, wisdom, energetic cleansing*

SANDALWOOD: *High spiritual vibrations, peace, strength, renewal*

STAR ANISE: *Luck*

## STRAWBERRY: *Luck, love*

Rose Quartz-Infused Sparkling Strawberry Lemonade, page 106

## TEA LEAVES

Green Tea: *Inspiration*

Astrological New Year Intention Setting Tea, page 92

Darkest Nights Tea for Turning Within, page 201

Inner Goddess Rosebud Tea, page 109

Black Tea: *Power, success, confidence*

Creativity Boosting London Fog Latte, page 229

Shadow Work Tea, page 188

Spiced Apple Chai for the Harvest Moon, page 176

The Magician Tea, page 121

White Peony Tea: *Intuition, calm*

Full Moon Tea for Reflection, page 52

Moonwater Sun Tea, page 130

Mugwort Dream Tea, page 239

Oolong Tea: *Reflection, wisdom*

Luminary Tea Blend for Community Support, page 149

## TEA TREE: *Creativity, protection, purification*

Candle Dressing Oil for Inspiration, page 96

Essential Oils for Hiking, page 196

## THYME: *Courage, health, sacredness*

Botanical Gin, page 168

Crystal & Herb Grid for Sacred Space, page 156

Herbed Honey Butter, page 142

Late Summer Harvest Sangria, page 143

## VALERIAN: *Deep sleep, dreams*

Dream Priestess Pillow & Sheet Spray, page 242

Mugwort Dream Tea, page 239

## VETIVER: *Banishing, balancing the spiritual and mundane*

Dream Priestess Pillow & Sheet Spray, page 242

Sacred Space Diffuser Blend for Daily Rituals, page 154

Waning Moon Bath Salts for Banishing Negativity, page 54

## WATERMELON: *Emotional cleansing*

Watermelon Sorbet for Emotional Cleansing, page 132

## WITCH HAZEL: *Purification*

Dream Priestess Pillow & Sheet Spray, page 242

Rosewater Facial Toner for Self-Love, page 102

Spring Cleansing Spray, page 93

Yoga Mat Cleansing Spray, page 203

## YARROW: *Spiritual protection, banishing*

Shadow Work Tea, page 188

Smoke Cleansing Bundle for Releasing, page 236

## YLANG YLANG: *Peace*

Bath Salts for Inner & Outer Balance, page 174